GRAND OBSERVATIONS

A Year of Weekly Visits to the Grand River at the Blair Road Bridge

Margie DeLong

To Don

Long run the river

Margie DeLong

FOR MY PARENTS
PAUL EDWARD DELONG AND RUTH MARIE CHARLES

"No American should go through life without knowing a river, some
river, and the wilder the better."
Wallace Stegner

CONTENTS

1 RIVER AND BRIDGE

Thursday, May 27, 2004, 8:15 p.m., 68° F.

I'm off to see the river – the most pristine one flowing into Lake Erie from either the United States or Canada. I desire something beyond work, family and house in my life. I want an activity that will keep me writing – I did not complete my last project. I was journaling about walking the Little Loop portion of Ohio's Buckeye trail, but Deb and I only completed eighty-seven of the 212 mile stretch before left knee pain grounded me.

The aptly named Grand River is only three and a half miles from my home. Although it's part of the scenery on my way to and from work, I often fail to notice it when crossing the Blair Road Bridge. But there the river is, wild and fairly unspoiled, ceaselessly flowing through LeRoy Township in Lake County on its way to Lake Erie. Today and weekly I will stop, stare and take photos. I will study this treasure that meanders through my township and county – this ancient topographical wonder bound to last for eons. I have no idea how much one can say about a river or if anything interesting will happen, but I aim to find out.

I snake down Blair Road, its south approach to the valley deliciously curvy, steep and wooded. The river only fully comes into view after passing a Tudor house on the sloping straightaway before the ninety degree turn onto the bridge. If you drive down the opposite side, it is obvious that a deep valley exists ahead as the roadway drops sharply and you can see over the treetops to the south valley wall. But the bottom remains hidden, even in winter, until you slow for the curve just before the bridge. The river, although expected, is, for me, an oh-h-h each time.

I am alone at the bridge – no cars, no human voices. Some birdsong wafts from the forested lowlands on this cloudy spring day, but it's mainly river talk that reverberates across the 500 foot wide valley to 200 foot high bluffs. I view the channeled water as it flows from the east around a peninsula of wooded lowland before straightening out at this bridge tucked along the south bluff. Downstream, a gentle northwest bend sends the river out-of-sight.

A lot of rain has fallen lately – great, fierce thunderstorms disgorging deluges. The Grand River accepts it all, temporarily overflowing onto its flood plains still intact on both sides of Blair Road about seven miles east of Painesville. Although I am too late for the highest water, the Grand River is still large, full and muddy, showcasing small trilling wakes at the bridge's center concrete support. The land around is lush with new-growth grass and rain-blackened tree trunks. A fine mist hangs at treetop height downstream and near the north bluff

1

upstream. How did this valley look before humans arrived – before the bridge and houses on the southeast bank and north rim? Even with today's occupants, enough beauty remains to delight me.

Just how grand is the Grand? Not that big when compared with the Mississippi, Nile, or Ganges rivers. But for our locale, it's the best thing in the neighborhood. Its ninety-eight and a half miles (or 102.7 miles on a few signs) with fifty-three named tributaries drain 455,680 acres. Although the Grand River is neither the shortest nor the longest river flowing into Lake Erie, it is more pristine and biologically diverse than any of the other U.S.A or Canadian rivers. To help preserve its attributes, fifty-six miles of the Grand River were designated Scenic (thirty-three miles) and Wild (twenty-three miles) by the Ohio Department of Natural Resources (ODNR) on January 17, 1974. My small view here at the Blair Road Bridge is part of the Wild section that begins at the Harpersfield Covered Bridge in Ashtabula County and ends at the Norfolk & Western railroad trestle south of Painesville in Lake County.

The ODNR's designation is based on quality, diversity, use, wildlife habitat and the level of human intrusion. Doesn't it give you pause when our species is considered a negative influence? For the Wild miles, there must be fully forested banks, little human invasion, high water quality, and healthy aquatic communities. The Scenic designation is given to portions less pristine in most of the categories. Ohio became the first state to enact Scenic Rivers. Now 683 miles of eleven rivers are designated such. Three rivers have earned national recognition from the U.S. Department of Interior – the Big and Little Darby creeks in the center of the state, Little Miami River in the southeast, and Little Beaver Creek a few counties south of here. Both state and national designations are often viewed by riverside landowners as too restrictive. So the fight goes on – how best to preserve nature and live there too.

Ohio must also claim a river which caught on fire on June 22, 1969. The infamous Cuyahoga River in Cleveland is the only Ohio river designated by the Environmental Protection Agency (EPA) as an American Heritage River, which helped cut corners to speed its recovery. Fishing and canoeing are summer activities again. How endearing can a city be where both a river and a mayor's hair caught on fire? Look the latter one up - his hair flamed twice while dedicating a bridge. I stand about forty miles east of that city and ten miles south of Lake Erie. I think I am at Wild mile seventy-eight from the Grand River's origin in southeastern Geauga County near Parkman.

I wish the homes were not here although I envy the residents. Two visible houses have windows facing the water. The Tudor one with small windows is about ten feet from the river on a twenty foot bank. The other building, about seventy-five feet east in the trees, has a wall of windows on the front of its A-frame. People living there hear river songs as well as rain symphonies on their tin roof. If either house ever comes on the market, I would have to inquire.

This metal through-truss bridge is the third or fourth one on Blair Road. A flood about 1860 washed away the original plank bridge. A covered bridge was next, valued for its strong barn-like construction and longevity since the supporting timbers were protected from the weather. The first covered bridge nationwide was built in 1805 in Philadelphia. The Blair Road Covered Bridge, the last of its kind in Lake County, was torn down in 1952. A steel erector-set bridge followed; later its sculptural sides were exchanged for low railings.

Wouldn't it be great to still see a covered bridge here? Few places have valued such a nostalgic, yet practical, bridge. Fortunately, the next county east, Ashtabula, has 15 drivable covered bridges. Each October there is a festival. And a new bridge is planned that will be the longest covered one in the country – that's country, not county. (The Smolen-Gulf Bridge, 613 feet across the Ashtabula River, opened for traffic on October 7, 2008. And then the county went on to build the shortest covered bridge in the country. The West Liberty Bridge – eighteen feet spanning Cowles Creek in Geneva – was ready for use on August 8, 2011. Now the count is 17.)

It's time to take my photos. I place my camera on a waist-high cement abutment for a view upstream. Turning forty-five degrees I view the bridge, its center cement pylon, and the water for my second shot. Across the road I do a vertical photo of the river flowing west against the south bluff, a maple tree's branches framing the left edge. Even when this tree is bare, greenery will be seen – an eastern hemlock crowds up behind. I have just enough light at 8 p.m. – the camera works. I plan to take my photos at the same three locations each week, although my visit won't be on the same day or same hour. But it's grand to have a plan. It's great to be still for a few minutes looking at the water. I'll be back and the river will be here.

East by northeast

West   North

2 A CANOE TRIP

Wednesday, June 2, 8:15 a.m., 58° F.

An early morning visit finds the Grand River within its usual channels. Islands of grasses, rocks, and semi-submerged logs upstream are flooded by sunlight that also lights everything north of the water. Shadows created by the high southern bluff stretch across the river to tree trunks now dry and light gray. The bridge's center column is mottled by sun and shade. Now that rocks are poking through the river's lower flow, the water's hum is disturbed by occasional burbling. No one else is here, no cars pass by; I alone watch sunlight caress the water and land.

The Whittlesey Indians (100-1650 AD) called this river "Sheauga Sepe"– Raccoon River. Whittlesey is the surname of the first European-American to study the Indians – whatever they called themselves has been lost. When French explorers arrived 300 years ago, hunting for a northwest passage, they renamed the river Le Grand Reverie. Sieur de la Salle was the first recorded European to cross the river.

Last weekend, we went down the river. My husband Colby and I, his brother Jan with his daughter Alicia, my daughter Heather and her friend Katie from Connecticut, all reserve kayaks at the Raccoon River Canoe Rental about 15 miles east in Harpersfield, Ashtabula County. We meet at the Harpersfield Covered Bridge, Ohio's current longest covered bridge at 228 feet spanning the wider of two dams on the Grand River.

There are two trips available. One starts farther east and ends just before the eight and one-half foot high dam. That run features a deep, muddy-bottomed river between farmland and woods. The trip we are taking has a shale-bottomed river running between bluffs and wooded flood plains like what is seen at the Blair Road Bridge. We may exit at either Hidden Valley Park or Mason's Landing. It is also the top half of the Wild section – the longest such river designation in Ohio.

Bob, the outfit employee, assures us the ride will be uneventful: "The water is mostly three feet deep, so most rocks are underwater. The rapids are fuller and rolling, which should make it easier to navigate." It's best to go in late spring before the water level drops to inches and one has to get out and push the boats around boulders. There has been so much rain this spring that Raccoon Run is hopeful of extending its season on this route long into summer. After signing the ubiquitous consent forms and listening to safety instructions, we put on our life jackets and shove off.

Although I have canoed before, I am a novice at kayaking and do a good bit of tipping and circling, splashing water on the kayak and me.

5

My calmer companions on straighter courses are soon all in front of me. The water is cold, the air not much warmer at sixty-two degrees even though it is noon on a June day. Fortunately, there isn't much of a breeze.

I manage to run into those stones that are not underwater. At one point I am wedged sideways, the river's force holding my kayak against a two foot wide boulder while everyone else continues downstream. Yelling "I'm fine," I struggle to get free using my paddle as a brace, then splaying my hand across the cold, slimy rock. Just before giving up and resigning myself to climbing out into the cold water, I shift my buttocks which moves the boat several inches. Ah, ha! After five big scoots and five big grunts, I am past the rock and on my way. I paddle rapidly (when no one ahead is looking) to catch up, acting nonchalant about my entrapment, although I can hardly swim the sidestroke (which I doubt would even work in the Grand River) and fear getting trapped underwater although it hasn't stopped me from rafting the Youghiogheny River in Pennsylvania (when I was younger) or going down the Colorado River in the Grand Canyon (on a motorized raft with guides).

For three hours we leisurely float on gently flowing waters or paddle through Class I and Class II rapids as rated by American Whitewater (their two mildest categories). We are not going through the Grand Canyon here, but the rapids are feisty enough to wet legs and feet. After the first hour the water feels warmer than the air. We float apart, paddle together, speak quietly, and silently point to great blue herons fleeing from our approach – their spread wings casting plane-like shadows on the water. We see basking turtles, a fleeing beaver, lots of bank swallows, and one Canada goose with three goslings.

Mile after mile we go downriver without seeing any houses except for the two at the County Line Road Bridge. Under fully leafed trees on the banks, some purple, mauve, and lavender phlox (I think) bloom, but the dames' rocket, an invasive species, looks similar. The sweet smell of locust blossoms wafts across the water. Occasionally vehicle noise from Interstate 90 (paralleling us in the north) is heard on a bend; otherwise, it's only nature sounds.

Only a few other people are out today. We pass a woman and two pre-pubescent children canoeists laughing and giggling while trying to maneuver downriver. Even I look accomplished next to them. Another party of four adults roasts hotdogs on the bank, smoke rising from their small fire. A fisherman in camouflage clothing at the river's edge becomes visible only when he surprises us by moving his fishing pole. He was as still as a standing blue heron.

I cannot believe how often I forget this place exists so close to my home. It's only my third time on the river since I moved to Lake County in 1974. I'm torn between raving about it or keeping this treasure a secret. At State Route 528, under the long, high bridge spanning Hidden Valley Park, we stop for a snack of nuts, raw vegetables, and grapes. On one of the bridge supports are black marker lines labeled in even numbers from two to 12. Have there been floods that reached the twelve foot line?

Colby complains of a backache (something about how he fits in the kayak); I am very cold (almost shivering). Jan (bless his heart) decides to join us in ending our journey here. Heather, Alicia, and Katie (the younger generation) will continue on to Mason's Landing at Vrooman Road. They will get to float under Blair Road Bridge with no idea of my weekly visits there. I am jealous and feel a bit wimpy. I always did the whole trip before, but the river-runners are coming back to our house for food along with other guests who couldn't or wouldn't kayak the river. Never mind that I'm getting older and more of my body protests sitting in a kayak so long. And it would be nice for three terrific young women to spend some time together. They plan to call on Katie's cell phone when they get to the Blair Road Bridge. What? I would never have thought to bring a cell phone on this trip.

I don't get a phone call. Colby suggests I just go to Mason's Landing, "They should be there by now." Good thing, too. I pick up three very cold but thrilled young women who immediately turn the car heater on high. I feel as if I am in a sauna by the time we get home, but they are just getting warm and rush off to take hot showers. A Grand River adventure ends and we all promise to do it again.

3 STONES AND EARTHQUAKES

Wednesday, June 9, 8:09 a.m., 76° F.

Spring rains are probably over. As the water recedes, the Grand River at the Blair Road Bridge shows its mud and gravel. Another row of rectangular stones forming the bridge's north support and embankment is visible. Did these same stones (fifteen rows high of rough-cut, stacked blocks fifty-two to fifty-six inches long, twenty-three inches high and twenty-four inches wide) support the prior covered bridge? Some stones are halved, one is missing, and one is by itself on the bank – victims of the river's might.

I find a black and white, undated picture of the Blair Road covered bridge in a 1996 Appointment Calendar published by the Lake County Historical Society. Yes, the stones look identical to the ones there now. The caption states the covered bridge connecting Perry and LeRoy townships was built c.1860. I am looking at chiseled stones that have supported three different bridges for 144 years – a span of seven successive human generations.

But the flood plains beyond the bridge in the photograph are markedly different from today – farm fields came up to both sides of a graveled Blair Road. How did they farm here with the spring and storm floods? Where forest exists on both sides of a now-paved road, trees back then only lined the last few feet at the riverbank or hugged the base of the north bluff. Those trees were small with few mature specimens – nothing to compare with the large, multi-trunked ones now towering over shrubs and brambles.

The south approach to the covered bridge in 1860 had rectangular stones too and a barren dirt roadway leaning toward the river. Those walls are now all cement and shrubs and grasses cover the upper half of the southeast bank above jumbled large rocks held in place by metal netting. Stability seems to have always been a problem where the river rubs against the curve.

Looking west today from the modern bridge, I see that the water has receded enough to reveal how the south bluff scoops at its base. High cumulus clouds overhead mute the greens of trees and grasses, gray the river and hide the sunlight. Warm air makes the fragrance fervid when compared with last week's visit. What a difference an eighteen degree rise in temperature can make.

How infrequently I think of the river, yet it continues to flow in the same spot, its gifts of movement, wildness, and water out of mind when out of sight. Just as I've become more aware of each day's weather, I want to have the Grand River in my mind more often. I want to carry the wetness of its water molecules in my spirit, hear its roaring or rippling or silence in my head and see its changing colors and volumes in my mind's eye.

But awareness is so mercurial. When my daughter Heather was a baby, I was amazed how easy it was to forget I now had a child. I once walked out of the house to go to the store and didn't remember my four-month-old baby until I got to my car. Talk about shock and guilt. As she grew and spent more time out of my sight, I got used to her absences. Eventually she left me and went all the way to Tierra del Fuego, Argentina, as a high school exchange student. The trepidation for her welfare never goes away; it just comes to mind less often. Time will tell how and when thoughts of the Grand River will arrive.

There's no accounting for thoughts of dead relatives. A word, a TV show, a flower and I'm recalling Grandma Glenna or Grandpa Wayne. I didn't think at their funerals that I would miss them; they were old, I was young. My parents, now in their eighties, are so much more often on my mind. I cannot imagine them not being present since they have always been here. But time will have its way. I also love serendipitous events that occur with relatives and friends that one hasn't thought of in months or years. "I was just going to call you." "I was thinking the same thing."

The Grand River seems to remain more the same than anything else in my life. It will continue flowing in its carved channel unless humans do something foolish or another geologic event changes its course like what happened when a new mouth for the Grand River emerged at Fairport Harbor before white settlement. Then the Grand River meandered close to the lake's shoreline for a mile or so through what is now the Mentor Marsh. But the old riverbank collapsed on one of its S-hook bends and formed a new outlet a few miles east. The vacated river channel filled with silt and became the lush marsh it is today. This 646.5 acre swamp with a stand of trees is Ohio's first interpretive nature preserve and was designated a National Natural Landmark in 1964. Every few years or so, the marsh catches fire, due usually to human carelessness or stupidity, and primal black smoke covers the land – a local disaster that nature speedily heals, compared to geological events that split, stripped, stirred, and reshaped the shores of one of the Mers Douce (Sweetwater Seas) as the Great Lakes were called by French explorers.

There have been more than 20 perceptible earthquakes since 1836 in northeastern Ohio. The strongest one (5.0 magnitude on the Richter scale) was on January 31, 1986. Movements from its epicenter in Lake Erie were felt primarily in Lake and Geauga counties. I was eating in a Painesville restaurant when the earthquake shook and boomed. The roof's snow cover fell off in one huge slide. Only when I saw the cooks leaving the gas stove kitchen did I go outside. It was not a truck running the nearby intersection and hitting the building, as some customers guessed, but my first earthquake.

Earthquakes here arise from a series of ancient faults three to six miles below in the crystalline rocks of the Precambrian age. The faults stretch northeast from Akron through Lake County and into Lake Erie. Plates shifting elsewhere cause a pressure build-up that is then released in weak faults. The bigger picture over time doesn't include you and me. At least for my lifetime, I can count on the Grand River seeming the same – unless there's 'the big one'. I can go to the Blair Road Bridge and record in photos its passage. I can sit on its banks and maybe see a bald eagle. (Each year in mid-January, volunteers do a bald eagle survey in Ohio. In 2007 a record 649 eagles were spotted. So far I've seen two eagles: one at Indian Point Park on the west edge of LeRoy Township, the other one over Ford Road which is two miles from my house.) At least for my lifetime, I can stick my hands and toes in the Grand River and feel its tug.

4 SLOWING DOWN

Monday, June 21, 5 p.m.

(I forgot to record the temperature. Later I tried to find it, but my patience was exhausted by the 3,169 Internet resources – many of which wanted money for the datum.)

Already my plan has hit a snag – it has been 12 days since my last visit. Last week I was on vacation in Mazatlan, Mexico. Today, after work, I stop at the Blair Road Bridge. Of course, the river is still here as is our house and all our relatives and friends. Nothing disastrous has happened while I was gone. Why do I never wonder if something marvelous will happen instead?

I feel disloyal though. While on vacation, I sat and watched Pacific Ocean sunsets every day at the Chiquita Banana Café – a silly name for a terrific restaurant perched above a lovely beach cove between the resort where we were staying and a hill locals climb to view sunsets. Four of us would arrive at the café around 7 p.m., order drinks and eventually dinner while watching from under a grass-thatched roof as the sun descended to the ocean. We would try to get a photo of the sun's touchdown and then stay until the moment of dark, which was always debated and impossible to pinpoint. I didn't think of the Grand River once.

Flying home at 15,000 feet by way of Houston, clear skies gave me great views of the large and muddy Buffalo Bayou wending its way through rectangular farm fields and rectangular housing subdivisions – where is our imagination? I did think of the Grand River then, wondering if its water level was up or down. I wish I could trace the length of the Grand River by airplane. Colby has a Cessna 172 stored at the Concord Airpark. He loves flying and has been disappointed that I don't share his enthusiasm for soaring on the wind. I love the soaring and the views but hate the noise. He's going to be delighted if I request to go flying over the Grand River.

I am reluctant to return to work. It's been so wonderful having days of Mexican food, an ongoing Scrabble tournament (Colby is ahead), swimming, reading, busing into the Sierra Nevada mountains, shopping for silver jewelry, and sleeping late. But I have a way to slow down from the hectic pace of modern life on my way to and from work – I drive at or below the posted speed limit.

The slower pace allows me to look for wildlife. A herd of deer often eats at the end of Pheasant Run, our neighbors' grass runway. Along my route I've seen possums, groundhogs, foxes, pheasants, vultures, crows and hawks along with LBJs ("little brown jobs") that I can't always identify. I watch for coyotes or bears that now reside in my township, making sudden stops to check out any movements in the woods.

Near the Grand River with its hilly roads, I am often the only car so my slower pace and pause on the Blair Road Bridge is not a problem. Drama begins at the end of Blair Road where I turn left onto River Road. This road is a favorite of car enthusiasts who like to try out sporty vehicles on its rises and dips. Any teenager with a new driver's license in Lake County knows about River Road. And so do the police.

The speed limit is 45 mph. I set my cruise control and often a car or truck is soon close behind me, hoping that the continuous yellow center line will change to a dotted one while I enjoy looking right and left at homes and hills. At one spot you can catch a glimpse of Lake Erie. This road, set upon the Madison escarpment, was once part of the lake's old shoreline. I like thinking the occasional boulders I see along the way may have once been splashed by Lake Erie waves.

At the end of River Road, I turn left onto State Route 84 and within a quarter mile make a right turn onto Madison Avenue. A right-on-red turn is allowed here, but it's an awkward intersection. Cars coming up the Vrooman Road hill on the left are not visible until the last moment, so I usually wait for the green light. I suspect drivers behind me are relieved when I turn away from the direction they are traveling.

The speed limit drops to 35 mph and so does my car. My head and hair look youthful from the rear, so a trapped driver cannot blame a little old lady for the pace. And if passed illegally, I find something to smile at so my developing jowls disappear. Meanwhile I am seeing manicured lawns with blooming lilies and trumpet vines. One property has a metal moose silhouette that the homeowners occasionally decorate with a neck scarf. There are wetland plants by the railroad tracks. Yes, I count the number of train cars if I get stopped at the tracks - I also turn off my engine, roll down my window and enjoy the sound of steel clanging and clunking over the rail seams.

When I deign to glance at my rearview mirror, I see tailgating, glaring, hand gesturing, and mouthed words. Five is the greatest number of vehicles lined up behind me so far. I know the drivers are in a hurry to get somewhere, but I wish for all of them a slower pace and just maybe a surprise if they notice what's around them. Even when a car passes me, I catch up at the next stop sign or traffic light, so what was the hurry for?

In Painesville I cross the Grand River again (and what a view here too) and climb the hill to Main and State streets. Only one block to go. I feel refreshed and ready for work. In only eight hours I get to leave work and drive home again at the speed limit.

When I stop at the Blair Road Bridge at the end of work today, the late-day sun is not visible above the valley's horizon, but its rays still shine on a stand of tree trunks free of branches for half their height on the river's northwest side. The shaded water intensifies the trunks' gold caste. All is still. The leisurely drifting river reflects the views around it, including some of the pale blue, partly-cloudy sky. I hear soft babbling at exposed rocks in the east. It's oh so pleasant, just me and the river. This way of slowing my pace down is even better than driving at the speed limit. Even the riverbed has a slow descent. Over its course the river drops only 544 feet, an average of five and a half feet per mile. I am five feet six inches tall. You could stack 97 of me at a 0.15 degree angle over the 254,130 feet of the river.

I've only discussed my weekly (well, almost weekly) project with my friend Dona in Virginia. Colby sees me writing but doesn't ask. I have an album where I place the three photos with a copy of that day's essay. When I flip the sheets back and forth, I already see how the river varies from week to week. I just need to figure out a way to manage vacations. Maybe I'll relent and clue in one other person so he/she can get photos for me when I am away – but then I wouldn't have seen the river. Best just to do as much as I can and let the rest go.

5 THE WAY OF WATER

Wednesday, June 30, 8:15 a.m., 70° F.

Summer has arrived. As I sit down to write this essay on my back porch, the temperature is 84 degrees F. A short rainstorm just passed – its dark blue clouds now northeast of the house. Sometimes I write my essay the day of my visit to the Grand River, but if not, at least within the week. I usually don't have more than five minutes to stay at the Grand River when I visit and I deliberately don't take notes so that I am not distracted from the view. I like recalling both the images and sensations later. I'm hoping they will stay with me longer that way and writing in the present tense helps with that process.

The Grand River looks summery too. The river has receded far off its banks. Gravel and sand bars stand out and direct the water's flow to the deeper portions of the channel. Although the bottom is mostly shale and shallow, it's a broad shallow waterway in a deep (by Ohio standards) valley. I suspect any kayakers or canoeists who come by now would have to push or pull their boats over rocks. This valley is generally left alone when the river's water is low except for traffic on the Blair Road Bridge, where once again I stand alone.

The river has its beginnings, according to the thin blue line on the Ohio map, somewhere north of Parkman and west of State Route 528 in Geauga County. I tell Colby about my desired plane ride and his eyes crinkle in delight. However, instead of starting somewhere out there at its beginnings, he suggests starting at Lake Erie and tracing it upstream. Clever man, my husband.

I think about this project a lot, thoughts of the Grand River coming up in the middle of a busy workday or while making dinner. I'm making a list of things to do. I hope to research any references to the Grand River on the Internet. I want to know about its current bridges and what happened to the old bridges whose remaining stone work is still seen here and there. Who are the lucky people who live within sight of the river? What groups are working to preserve this state-designated Wild and Scenic gem? What is it like to sit silently for an hour at the river's edge?

A year may not be long enough to find the answers since I work fulltime, but hallelujah, recent budget cuts at the non-profit agency where I work have helped. All the staff voted to work one day less per week in hopes of saving all workers' positions. This is perfect – a day each week for my writing. It's a dream come true. And because I've opened my mouth so many times about wanting to write, it's time to do so.

Accompanying my writing today are randomly croaking frogs in a small pond visible from my dining room window. For 17 years I have had the pleasure of this manmade but naturally developed water feature at a cost of $500 ($816.99 in today's dollars). It was the best money I ever spent. My only regret is that I didn't keep a journal about it. It feels right to be writing about the Grand River next to a body of water which I named Rana Pond (Spanish for frog).

My five and one-half acres are only .0012% of the Grand River watershed which has an outline resembling Africa. The river looks like a squiggly seven with a shoe at the bottom and a crumbled, upturned hat brim at the top. My little pond is not even a dot in this illustration (Appendix A). Most of the rainwater falling on my property returns to the Chardon Thin Upland Aquifer, an underground layer of porous rock and water which my well reached at fifty-five feet. Some of the rain makes it all the way to the Grand River when the soil is water-logged. Run-off on my road's ditches flows into an unnamed creek two properties away, then west to Paine Creek before running north to the Grand River. And here's a fact for you – a drop of water in Lake Erie spends six years there before leaving by way of Niagara Falls. How was that figured out?

The water quality of the Grand River is the best of any river that flows into Lake Erie because of the riparian areas along its banks. The width of these desired corridors is set by local officials based on the size of the watershed. Buffers of natural vegetation and flood plains vary from twenty-five feet on each side for small streams up to 120 feet or more for larger rivers and watersheds. Riparian corridors reduce the severity of floods, filter and settle pollutants, and protect terrestrial and aquatic habitats. Trees at the rivers' edges regulate water temperatures by providing shade.

But increased human habitat results in storm runoff from impervious surfaces, increasing the river's peak flows, causing more erosion, and threatening structures that were once thought to be safe. Currently, any new subdivision in LeRoy Township is subject to setback requirements. It would be better if that included any new building by anyone. Of course, any existing buildings within the adopted setback area are grandfathered. We just have to wait for them to fall into the river or hope the landowner sees value in removing them or at least not replacing them after flooding occurs.

In the end it's all about having enough quality water for all species which is part of what makes the Grand River such a plum. Today I watch its endless flow of brown water pass between the summer-green plains of mature trees and the high shale bluffs' gray/brown layers under an overcast sky, grateful for its meandering ways.

6 CLOUDS AND BARN DOORS

Friday, July 9, 11:00 a.m., 68° F.

I forgot to get my camera out of the Honda before Colby took it to Pittsburgh and left me the Sable. We both love the Honda and hope it's the one we get to drive, but it does make sense to use it for business trips because it's newer and gets better gas mileage. I've been storing my camera between visits to the river in the cubbyhole (as my father calls the glove department) so it will be there when I need it. And it IS there in the Honda, but I'm driving the Sable – which finds me at the river without a camera.

The amount of time I spend looking and searching for desired objects because I can't remember where I last left them has increased exponentially with my age. Notes, mnemonics, and routines have become my focus. It bothers me to waste time hunting for stuff when I could be reading or writing or sitting by Rana Pond. My octogenarian parents make me more conscious of minutes. Many minutes seem mundane, but that is all right. Life is, as the Buddhists say. I will have to come back again this week to take my photos.

Today, halfway down Blair Road's southern hill, I see two vehicles parked on the right side. One is a car with a canoe strapped to the top; the other a van with Case Western Reserve University lettered on the driver's door. A middle-aged woman is getting out of the van to meet the man already outside the car. Um – a clandestine rendezvous? I read too many novels. No, I need time to read more of them.

I drive past and park in my usual spot just beyond the driveway of the Tudor house. There's just enough room between the end of their driveway and the guardrail leading to the bridge – even the Sable fits. So I don't have to go on to a pull-off 500 feet north of the bridge. Here at my preferred parking place I am twenty-five feet from the river.

It's partly cloudy today. I wonder what the difference between partly cloudy and partly sunny is. Seemingly simple terms, I bet the descriptions are heavily codified so the atmospheric labels make sense to meteorologists. For one of my tasks at work the terms white, whiter, and whitest are used. The designations seemed impossible at first but now I use them with confidence. Yes, I would say today is partly cloudy since there is more sun space in the sky than clouds – with apologies to the American Meteorological Society.

It's a little cool for midday in July. The river trills softly around gravel beds and rocks, its water level low. A fallen tree trunk on the right side is totally exposed. It was deposited there before my attentions, probably by a spring's flood. When will it continue its journey? At this moment the sun is partially visible. Partly lit? Partly dark?

As I'm pondering over words, the canoed-car with both the man and woman inside drives slowly by and over the bridge. Getting a second glance at them, they look like stereotypical university professors from the 60's. Long gray-streaked hair is bound by a rubber band at her nape. His hair is shorter but touches the collar of a well-worn khaki shirt. They look like people who spend a lot of time outdoors. There's no conversation between them, no laughing – they are checking me out. I bet they are some type of -ologist here to study my beloved Grand River. Carry on with your science and enjoy the fine day.

What would make this moment even better is if the 150 foot long covered bridge still existed. *Here Is Lake County, Ohio* relates an adventure at the Blair Road Covered Bridge in 1918:

"...the County Commissioners felt the pressure of modern life sufficiently to allow the County Engineer the time-saving device of using a taxi when he had any extensive trip to crowd into a day. So one fine morning, the Engineer and his assistant started off in a model T Ford with a greenhorn from the city at the wheel. They inspected ditches and culverts in Concord and Leroy and in the late afternoon started for home. The driver had about all the scenery he needed and all the bumpy, dusty roads. He lit out for Painesville.

The car was going at a good clip when it arrived at the top of Blair Hill. It slithered down around one curve after another, scarcely slowing, bumping from one rut to the next. The two men in the back seat clutched their straw hats with one hand and with the other clung to any bracket they could reach. Suddenly, the driver slammed on the brakes and skidded to a shivering halt on the clanking boards of the covered bridge. "Whew!" said our hero, mopping his brow, "It certainly was lucky them barn doors were open!"

The replacement bridge on Blair Road, constructed in 1952, had all steel girders in a cross hatch pattern with the sides reaching eight feet in the center before tapering down at each end. The river was easily seen between the green painted uprights and braces, which were great to grasp when one leaned out to scan the water. Even though it wasn't a covered bridge anymore, this construction wasn't a modern bridge. I liked that.

Lake County replaced this erector set bridge with a new, low-sided metal-railed one in 2003. The first time I crossed the new bridge, I was thrilled. The railings were only twenty-eight inches high. Nothing obscured my line-of-sight, allowing a full view of the Grand River from my car. But after having the taller sides for so long, it felt as if I could roll right over into the water even though I knew the rails were sufficient. Evidently other travelers were more disconcerted. Citizens complained and a second railing was installed, adding sixteen more inches. This railing is exactly in my line-of-sight. Once again I have to stop and get out of the car to fully see the river.

When I return the next day for my photos, it is sunny. I snap views of the bridge embankment with its old stones and a grove of trees farther west perfectly reflected in the slow, soundless river. Today seems exactly like yesterday but of course, it's not. Different water flows under the bridge, the temperature is not the same, the air is thicker or thinner, the skies are clear. I don't have time at this moment to ponder. This mundane moment with its nuances just is.

7 NIGHT VISIT

Monday, July 12, 10:15 a.m., 70° F.

It's been raining a lot lately –unusual for July in Ohio. In Europe it has been one of the coldest summers. Our newspaper had a picture of snow on a picnic table in Italy. When I see the river this Monday, nothing seems changed from the week before – same gravel bars and rocks although cumulus clouds are gathering above the hilltops. But when I look closely, I see that vegetation covering the old stones on the northeast embankment is fuller and the woods beyond seems darker and less penetrable.

Does anything watch me watching the Grand River? No birdsong or breeze at this moment. I don't have time to wait for something to happen, but the forests are breathing, photosynthesizing beside the steady movement of water next to their roots. I, who can't see those actions, will live a shorter time compared with the trees. With lots of time, I might be able to see many species along the Grand River: 74 fishes, 115 birds, 45 mammals, 18 reptiles, 10 amphibians, and 60 rare plants. Included among these are the reintroduced river otter, wild turkey, snowshoe hare and the white-tailed deer (a huge success). I love plant names like spotted touch-me-not, sensitive fern, Jack-in-the-pulpit, and cut-leaf toothwort. I am familiar with the green heron, wood duck, red-tailed hawk, northern harrier, and pileated woodpecker. They visit my home too, as do spotted turtles, leopard frogs, and American toads – just a small sampling of what the river enjoys.

And I'm on the lookout for black bear here and at home. The number of sightings in Ohio has gone from 66 in 2000 to 165 in 2002. In the summer, bears probably follow Interstate 90 from Pennsylvania to Ohio for food and habitat before heading back for the winter. However, the Ohio Division of Wildlife estimates that about 24 bears live in Ohio year round.

Our house was reroofed this week. Blue tarps covered my flower beds along the sides of the house. Torn asphalt tiles and tar paper flew down from the roof - nightmare precipitation. I rushed out to grab a couple of pieces that fell in Rana Pond. Then it rained, and rained, and rained. Water seeped in one kitchen window before the workers put tarpaper on the exposed plywood. I didn't get a glimpse of the Grand River until the weekend. By then all the rain had been absorbed into the thirsty ground and any rise of water volume at the river was gone. One of these days I'll get to the river for a storm surge.

It was a busy weekend. We motored to Mansfield for my father's family reunion. Cousins, who hadn't attended in years, showed up, just when I thought interest was waning. Now I will have to get back to work on those genealogy charts. Colby and I came back Saturday to attend Painesville's Party in the Park. A friend had said the best local Latin jazz band would be playing at 10:30 p.m. We went, we saw, we heard. And the band, Roberto Casio's Latin Jazz Project, was good.

One purchased CD later, we are on our way home down Blair Road. On the bridge, Colby stops the car, opens its windows, turns off the headlights and shuts off the motor (I introduced this practice to him). Suddenly the river, passing inaudibly under the bridge, is ours and only ours. A mist formed by the night's cooler temperature lies above the water under a dark and cloudy sky. The surrounding bluffs and trees are barely seen. In silence, we breathe intently. I lose sense of Colby, the car, the road; my being is attuned to the everlasting river. We should do this more often.

Tonight no oncoming cars hasten our departure. Sometimes, especially when we choose to get out of the car and stand along the bridge rails, we have to scramble to avoid being discovered if a vehicle comes. Our slamming doors seem out of place then when we start the engine, flip on headlights and try to move before the approaching car arrives on the bridge. Safety is important but I also want to preserve our secret stop. I don't want to share this brief moment of pleasure from this large river. Go and find your own special place and I hope it includes a river.

And on this Monday in daylight at the Blair Road Bridge with the cloud-shaded water snaking through this beautiful valley, the memory of our night visit reminds me how little I know about this Grand River - even this specific spot.

8 SITTING STILL

Saturday, July 24, 8:13 a.m., 68° F.

Emmett, our gray-striped American shorthair cat, wakes me up. Once he hears one of us stirring as daylight starts to appear, he jumps on the bed, stands next to a head, purrs loudly, and licks any accessible body part. I ache anyway from the night's rest, so up I get. Osteoarthritis in my left knee and neck gets me tossing and turning and hot flashes dictate the flinging off and pulling on of blankets. And if I nose-snore (not throat, which is much worse and what someone else does), Colby touches my shoulder until I roll on my side. So a good night's sleep is one in which I hear the clock strike the hours only on two occasions.

When I come downstairs, the sunlight is brilliant. Yesterday had been cloudy, but today bright light is streaking across Rana Pond and splashing off the yellow daylilies at the split rail fence. Colby gets up a few minutes later. I announce my departure for the Grand River but arrive four minutes too late to claim the earliest time thus far. Some morning I should set my alarm clock for dawn.

No one is at the river. The people who live in the Tudor house have not picked up their newspaper yet. I hear the water's whispering ripples; I breathe in the morning air, consciously exhaling longer than usual as I study the shadows and reflections. The morning light makes an open funnel of the eastern bend and a dark tunnel of the western river curve. Only the treetops here are struck by sunlight.

Which way would I choose to go if I happened upon this place for the first time and had to make my way out of here? The original Indian inhabitants, now called the Whittlesey culture, were named after Charles Whittlesey, an assistant Ohio geologist who discovered numerous Native American earthworks in the late 1930's statewide survey. I have no idea if he ever visited this valley, but after several decades of geological work, he helped establish the Western Reserve Historical Society in 1867, serving as its president until his death on October 18, 1886. Whittlesey is a nice enough name, certainly not Smith or Jones, but I still would like to know what the natives called themselves.

I almost stopped yesterday to spend an hour by the riverside, but a truck was parked in the north pull-off. I want the river to myself for that experience. And sitting still for an hour may be more of a challenge than I anticipate. I found that out yesterday afternoon when I was on my back deck reading *The Big Year* by Mark Obmascik. A great blue heron coasted in for a landing at the west end of Rana Pond just fifteen feet away. It strolled along the pond's edge before flying to the top railing of the split-rail fence. I stayed still and stared. The frogs had splashed and disappeared underwater as soon as the bird alighted. I determined to stay still as long as the bird remained.

It took concentration and subtlety. First, my left knee started throbbing. If I flexed my foot, I gained a minute or two of relief. Then my shoulders started to hurt. Well, no wonder, I had them bunched. My right hand holding the book went numb. I did manage to lower the book to my lap and remove my hand without disturbing the bird. The heron was stiller than I was; only cocking its head now and then with no seeming correlation to surrounding sounds – at least the ones I am creating.

I heard Colby coming down the stairs. Oh, no, he's going to come out on the porch. I held up my right hand, hoping my waving fingers would catch his attention. But as soon as he opened the screen door, the heron took flight. Its broad gray-blue wings filled the gap between the trees beyond the fence as the bird seemed to float on the tops of the understory shrubs. The bird never rose up into the sky, but perched nearby out of sight, only to return about an hour later. We were inside the house this time and watched until it left for good of its own volition – just when Colby was sneaking around the house for a photo. At least I got some practice before I sit still at the Grand River.

I would stay longer by the river today, but Colby is making breakfast. And part of that breakfast will be leftover homemade cherry pie. Talk about a perfect start to a Saturday. I have communed with the Grand River and now can have my piece of pie.

9 FIRST HOUR SIT

Wednesday, July 28, 1:15 p.m., 63° F.

I do it. After taking my usual three photos, I re-park my car in the pull-off at the base of the north bluff. I plan to walk through the woods to the Grand River and spend an hour sitting on its bank. There seems to be a trail snuggled next to the steep shale bluff. Fishermen park here all the time, so this must be their route to the water instead of walking down the road to climb over the guardrail just before the bridge and descend the steep embankment.

I start off into the woods but the trail rapidly narrows. The light dims. This must be an animal path because it leads me into blackberry vines and wild rose brambles. I'm surprised I cannot hear the river from here, but all is quiet except for a few bird calls and breeze-scuttled leaves high overhead. I'm not lost - how could I be in a few acres bounded by a road, a bluff, and a river – but I don't appear any nearer to my goal. The filtered sunlight is not enough to warm me, but my scrambling does.

After eating a few berries and scanning the ground for signs of bear tracks, I tediously angle back toward the road. Thorns grab my clothes and low-lying branches brush my face. When I stop to admire a beech and swat my first mosquito, I see, just before the road embankment, a large swale that appears well-trodden and free of undergrowth. Is this path created by water run-off, humans or animals? I'm back to thinking about bears.

According to the experts at the Ohio Division of Wildlife, if you meet a bear "… stay calm, do not try to escape by climbing a tree – it can climb, too – or try outrunning an animal that can move at 35 mph." Okay, now I know what not to do, but what do I do? "Back away slowly, facing the bear and leaving it ample room to get away." I'm in a thick forest with brambles and on possibly the only clear path in the immediate vicinity. "If attacked, stand your ground, raise and wave your arms to make yourself seem bigger, shout, fight back with whatever is at hand." My water bottle? "…the chances of being killed by lightning are greater than being slain by a black bear." Slain!

Boldly moving forward in the swale, I come upon an obvious trail about five feet before the bridge leading from the road's guardrail directly to the water. I'll bet those fishermen don't walk through the woods at all but come here instead. It's a little steep for the first ten feet but I make it down to the grasses beside the river. I don't regret my roundabout route; now I know what is and what wasn't in there today.

I move northeast along the river's edge to a log, which looks as if it's been here several years. Its bark is mostly gone and the underlying smooth wood has silvered. The cleansed root ball is on my left as I face the river. As the trunk becomes smaller, it splits into two branches, one angled toward the bank and the other toward the bridge, giving me a perfect perch and backrest. I snap five or so photos, and then settle down to begin my hour at the river by 1:30 p.m. No speaking, no writing – just observing.

It's a cloudy, cool day. The river flows by at about two to three miles per hour, foam dollies on its smooth surface. The water is low enough that gravel beds are visible on both sides of the river and protruding rocks in the middle create enough disturbances to make the smallest of rapids at the bend to my right. Its swishing riffle is soothing, almost drowning out the noise of occasional cars traversing the Blair Road Bridge. I can see only one of the white and brown gables of the Tudor house. Halfway up the southern hill directly opposite the bridge, the gray-brown siding and deck of another home built there within the past five years is visible. Otherwise all is lush green grasses and shrubs under mature trees that fill the valley land before climbing some of its walls.

For thirty minutes I am entranced by the water's flow and a flock of bank swallows dive-bombing for insects. Crows caw overheard and a pair of ducks flies downstream beneath them. Even the light rain is welcome as it makes thousands of minute splashes on the water. I put on my windbreaker and open the umbrella. It's just me and the river with an occasional passing car's whoosh on the bridge muffled by the rain's soft plopping. (I do not mention hearing bells – which you will learn about later – maybe they were not tolling that day.)

At 2 p.m., a canoe and a kayak, each carrying one soaked man, come into view on my left. "Where did you come from?" I call out. "From the county line. Is there a path to the road by the bridge?" I know the answer to that one and call out when to aim for the bank. The nice thing about meeting people passing on the river is that the length of conversation is set by the speed of the water.

I watch them pull ashore just before the bridge and drag their river conveyances up the steep bank and presumably over the guardrail – trees and the river's bend hides them now. After fifteen minutes of banging and indistinct voices, I hear car doors slam. There wasn't a parked car here when I arrived. Someone must have come to meet them.

I'm alone again. The rain has stopped. I find my mind wandering onto work concerns (but it's the first time this hour) and deliberately focus again on the swallows and water. I try to trace just one swallow's flight but lose it quickly among the erratic flock. At 2:30 p.m. I stand, use up my roll of film, walk to the swale through knee-high grass laden with water drops, climb over the guardrail, and return to my car. A park ranger's car is now there too. I hear thrashing across the road and walk over to see what's going on just in time to greet the ranger struggling up the embankment.

"What are you doing?" I ask. (This is not a park, so what would he have to do here? Maybe he heard about a rare plant. Who does own this river bottom?)

"Just looking around and trying to get up this hill. What are you doing?" he replies.

Proudly I respond, "I was sitting by the river." Silence, no response to what I thought would reassure him or maybe pique his interest. At least he says goodbye before getting into his car and heading uphill. Only then do I think he may have been using 'outdoor facilities' on his patrolling route through my township to nearby Paine Falls and the Hell Hollow Wilderness Area.

Turning my car around, I stop just before the bridge and climb out with a plastic bag just as the park ranger's car comes back down the hill. He stops.

"I'm going to pick up all these beer cans someone threw here by the path," I say.

"Thanks," he says, then drives on over the bridge.

As I move toward the swale, I see a kayak pushed down by a tree. The river travelers must have had room for only one craft atop that car. Hmm, my daughter has always wanted a kayak (this one is a lovely forest green) and the park ranger has made his rounds. What am I thinking? I barely got myself up and down this bank, let alone a kayak. Besides, the first suspect would be the mature woman in soaked hair and turquoise Capri pants carrying a red, blue, and white umbrella to the silver Honda Accord as recalled by the park ranger who was almost caught in the middle of his 'break'.

10 RIVER PARTS

Thursday, August 5, 10:15 a.m., 64° F.

This last week, two inches of rain fall over two days. My rain gauge dutifully records the event, Rana Pond fills to its brim, and the frogs disappear until the sun comes out. Once again I miss getting photos of a big flow at the Grand River.

After pestering him for two weeks to just get the job done, I help Colby put a tin roof on the storage shed and build a wooden platform for my green plastic composter. I announce that we are not tackling any new projects until we complete the ones already in progress. The Slanty Shanty needs its insides insulated and walled in old boxcar siding. I want another tin roof on top of its tar paper so I can rush out there when it rains and sit on a bench under the overhang until mosquitoes drive me inside to my writing desk and chair – which needs its cane bottom re-weaved.

And we both want to add a bump-out in the house at the bottom of the stairs. The space between the last step and wall is narrow and dark – the building was first a garage. Any expanse of blank wall and I want to add a window. Jan, Colby's architect brother, came up with a clever idea for a triangular space with windows on two sides and a seat ledge overlooking my trellised garden. But all must wait for projects already in progress or our property will begin to look like others I've seen where I make judgments about the owners' capabilities. "They never seem to finish anything, do they?" Meanwhile, I have the Grand River to visit.

I did see it on Monday on my way to work. The water was higher, brown, flowing fast and covering where I walked last week and halfway up the log where I sat. But my camera was at home again and I am out of film. When I work in Painesville, I cross the river again on Main Street with great views on both sides of the bridge. There's also one spectacular tree on the southeast corner. It has five large trunks rising up from the ground – it's some kind of willow. Someday I am going to stop, measure, and photograph it. Work gets in the way as does my low energy after work. I just want to stay in my cozy house once I get there. Mornings are my high energy times but the problem is getting up early enough for an activity before work. Reading the newspaper while drinking a cup of tea is more attractive.

But the good news is my four-day work week. My paycheck is smaller, but time is more important – time to try all the stuff I've talked about for years – writing essays, crafting poems, plotting a mystery, researching genealogy, studying photography, practicing the piano, watching the weather and birds. And time to make a grape flan from my ripening wild grapes which I trained by selective pruning and tying. Peeling and seeding grapes connects me to the sun's pulse and the porosity of my fingertips.

Going home after work, I can just catch a glimpse of the river far below when I'm at the top of the Madison Avenue hill heading east (which is what Main Street becomes). The road at a bluff's edge overlooks a vast valley of water and trees, but there is no place to park. Here the Grand River makes several huge bends before heading into downtown Painesville. I want to walk down there, but there is no path that I know about. Wouldn't it be grand to have a walking trail along the entire length of the river?

The Grand River basin is divided into four sections: headwaters, lowlands, gorge and estuarine. The headwaters flow through primarily agricultural lands with spaced farms. The lowlands, site of an ancient glacial lake, are also sparsely populated and the river moves slowly over a muddy and silt-covered bottom past some of Ohio's largest wetlands, flood plain forests, marshes, wet meadows, and swamps.

The gorge section has escaped major development so far due to its rugged hills and steep valleys. The visible river on my way to work is in this portion. The roads I take wander on and off the bluffs through rural and urban areas. The valley views are marred by high tension towers in Painesville and some unshielded lights at night. I'd prefer that nothing stick above the trees nor any light source be visible. However the houses perched on the bluffs above the serpentine crawl of the Grand River through the wide valley in Painesville look postcard-perfect from a distance. A newer beige water tower seems out-of-place compared to the weathered wood and metal one still standing farther south.

Unfortunately the estuarine area was lost long ago. It starts when the banks of the river broaden and flatten near the train trestle by State Route 84 Bridge in Painesville and ends where the river meets Lake Erie's small tides. All along this section there used to be broad wetlands and mudflats. Now it is highly urbanized with dense population, commercial and industrial enterprises, and all the trappings of water recreation. Although the Ohio EPA states that aquatic life in Painesville has improved over the years and meets its healthy-level criteria, the waste ponds near the Diamond Shamrock lagoons are still emptying hexavalent chromium into the Grand River. The EPA recommends a 40 percent reduction to meet water quality standards. That's a huge amount. Is it just improvement of past impairments that guide the actions? Obviously, there is much more work to be done, and wouldn't it be great to see more mudflats and wetlands along the estuarine section?

Today, I am finally organized and ready to take my photos. At the Blair Road Bridge, the water has receded and the bank grass is matted and pale where it was recently underwater. If I had been at my log seat during the high water, my feet and legs would have been underwater. More likely, I would have been swept downstream and drowned. The small rapids are gone. Now a sonorous, rumbling, solid tongue of brown water scours the banks, just barely giving way at the cement support holding up the bridge. The river's speed upsets my equilibrium – I grasp the bridge railings. All is draining into Lake Erie. There will be more rainstorms and another flow of the river over the bent grasses at its sides. Maybe I will catch the river's play then.

July 28 Hour Sit Perch

11 THREE MORE PARKS

Beaty Landing – March 18, 2009

A new park has been established along the Grand River in Painesville within walking distance for its citizens. Opened October 24, 2007, it's just fifty-four acres, but located on the flood plain (or is it a flood zone) between the bluffs on which Madison Avenue, State Street, and Walnut Street run. The wooded wetland has a mile long, graveled loop trail with three shorter river access paths along its 3,300 feet of river frontage. I finally visit it on my way home after visiting the staff at Grand River Partners, Inc.

(This is what happens when you look things up. Everything I've been calling a flood plain is probably a flood zone, or more likely a combination of both. Land formed along a river from sediment deposited there by floods is a flood plain. Flood zones are lands inundated by 100 year flooding and the First American Flood Data Services has six pages of categories for them. Henceforth, everything is a flood zone in this book because that is more likely, but I like the sound of flood plain more and there have been floods along the Grand River.)

I am alone as I amble down the Walnut Street bluff past an overlook deck up top and a park bench suitably placed halfway down. I may need to rest there when I climb back up this hill. The view over the valley extends north to the houses on Madison Avenue. Although it looks like rain, there is some sun.

When I reach the flatlands, I must choose which way to go around the oval loop. I go right, where the park abuts another large parcel of river bottom land that I fervently hope is also protected from development. Birdsong comes from all directions as I pass between tall deciduous trees. Traffic hum from the bluff roads fades in and out. It is delicious to be in town and yet in a wild area with only one trail. I wander down each of the three river access paths as I come to them. The river is at least seventy-five to one hundred feet wide in an oxbow and about five feet deep. At places silent and other spots gurgling, the river can be seen and touched, but I wouldn't swim (nor is it allowed) in this strong current. What a jewel of a park this is with its river views and undisturbed woods.

I discover at the end of the oval trail a park sign with colored drawings of the fish that can be caught here: blue gill, black and white crappie, largemouth and smallmouth bass, bullhead, channel catfish, walleye, yellow perch, brown and steelhead trout, and pumpkinseed – what a great fish name. What about a sign about birds? No, no – no more signs. How about a notebook where birders could record bird species seen? Heading back up I pass a man and woman starting down the hill.

Baker Road Park – October 13, 2012

Hurrah, the Metroparks successfully purchased some of the auctioned land in LeRoy Township. Colby and I had walked the property when the auction notice appeared and saw how the parents had created a wonderland of paths and stone bridges for their children. The western section was flat and on a high bluff over the Grand River before the hills, ravines, and waterfalls in the midsection led to an old roadbed going downhill to the lowlands at the Grand River. I had sent an email to Lake Metroparks – wanted to be sure they knew the land was up for sale. They (or should I say, we, the citizens) now own 76 acres that includes part of the deep ravine with its twenty foot waterfall, the old roadbed and flatland beyond. A narrow corridor allows access off Baker Road onto the 0.62 mile minimally-improved trail.

Walking there today I am surrounded by mature trees in their pre-winter skeletal beauty. Birds sing gaily as I peruse the ravine and find the waterfall just beyond an old-growth maple. A meadow on my right was where we meet one of the adult children and his family who were camping one more time before the sale. "We hate to see the land go, but none of us live close by and can afford to buy out the others," he said.

Going downhill, I stop to admire again and again some old growth trees. A small pond waits at the base of the hill. There's a new footbridge over the creek and then it's a short walk to the edge of the Grand River. Today the flow is full and strong. I am rewarded with a large splash after my ten minutes of contemplation.

The park's website states 30 species of birds, five species of butterflies, and four species of dragonflies have been spotted here, not to mention the chance of beaver dams built on the floodplain (their choice of word). I plan to come back here often. I had the place to myself and it's less than 4 miles from my house.

River Road Park – 2012

On the north side of the river farther east, these 10 acres have been opened to the public. A 0.75 mile mowed grass trail leads past a pond (fishing is permitted) onto a natural overlook of the Grand River. The pond is stocked with bass, bluegill and catfish. Hurrah, another place to explore and view a section of the Grand River valley and its river. And it's less than 10 miles from my house.

12 OVERHEAD VIEW

Saturday, August 7, 10:41 a.m., 60° F.

The sky is robin's egg blue with cumulus clouds and strong sunlight. "Let's go fly the river," Colby says. "It's better flying in the morning. The air's less bumpy." I grab my sunglasses, notebook, pen and camera. Off we go to Concord Airpark, where he hangars his Cessna 172. This will be my second chronicle in one week, but, oh, well. You have to grab adventure when it's offered.

After flying north for ten miles we are over the mouth of the Grand River on Lake Erie near the eastern village of Fairport Harbor. A large sand and gravel company sits on the west bank. That probably explains the fan-shaped milky, pale green water extending a short distance into the lake before the aqua, then blue colors.

First we circle, which takes us over a relative's home in a new housing development east of Fairport Harbor on Lake Road. They have a panoramic view of Lake Erie out their dining room windows that will eventually be compromised as more houses are built, but for now, I am jealous of their lake views.

"Hey, they've got their patio built. We need to wangle an invitation," I shout. Small planes are great for getting close-up earth views, but ear protectors are a must. Communication means lifting one ear cover after saying huh several times or shouting or trying hand signals. This is no time for charades.

Seeing the river from above is thrilling, even if I am seeing it backwards; while we are flying to its origin, it is flowing to its end at Lake Erie. I see how its southward, upstream path quickly turns back toward the lake and then west toward the city of Painesville. South of town the river makes a huge semicircle before heading east through four Lake County townships – Painesville, LeRoy, Perry, and Madison. The river is a giant brown snake slivering through dark green bands of trees with many, many bends and several oxbows, their U-shapes clearly visible from the air.

I know the river bends south again in Ashtabula County. In Trumbull and Geauga counties, it turns west one more time before finally petering out somewhere above the town of Parkman. The exact beginning of the river is still a mystery. Tim Warsinskey (a Cleveland *Plain Dealer* writer) set out in 1998 to find its headwaters - the small streams that join to form a river. He found himself eventually surrounded by trickles of water at the edge of a bean field in Geauga County's Amish farmland. (*Geauga, a Magazine for the County*, spring 2008, reports the Grand River starts in Parkman Township, near the Boy Scout

Camp Chickagami, and that most of the Grand River's headwaters are in Geauga County. Grand River Partners now has an agricultural easement on the Irwin farm which is near the headwaters. Deciding which creek in this area starts the river is a conundrum.)

Land use in the Grand River watershed is 52.6% forested, 39.5% agricultural, 6.5% water/wetlands, and only 1.4% urban. When you consider that only a half century ago, only 12% of Ohio's land was still forested, we are not doing too badly here in northeast Ohio. Our 52.6% forested land is above the 30% Ohio average. I would have loved to have seen Ohio (o-y-o as the Shawnee called it) when it was mostly forested and richly endowed with wetlands. We humans do have a knack for knocking the heck out of things.

As we continue on, there is rarely a straight river section. I don't want to miss any view of this magnificent behemoth beneath us, but it's a struggle to keep the river in sight. We can't fly on top of it because we can't see through the bottom of the plane; we have to fly off to one side or the other. When the river turns, the plane cannot bank as readily, hence we circle instead, again and again.

I haven't been up in his plane for months and my body reacts with a headache and mild nausea. Colby shouts, "Focus on the top of the dashboard," which helps. So I alternate between viewing the river and viewing the instrument panel. I try taking photos but I doubt any of my three shots will be useful. I stubbornly insist on using my Kodak Advantage F600 with its Ektanar Aspheric lens even though Colby offered me his Cannon A1A with telescopic lens. I want to be consistent throughout my project – even when it doesn't make sense?

We fly mostly at 2,500 feet. I count 25 bridges along our course, two of which are train trestles and three of which are covered bridges. Farmed fields or homes stretch to the edge of the wood lining the banks. There's one golf course and one swimming pool, but it's mostly woods, fields or homes. I barely see the Blair Road Bridge nestled among the trees when we pass by. I like how it's so protected by its bluffs and treed flood zones. I like how it's a small part of the landscape when seen from the air. I like how I stop every week to view and photograph it.

The high banks seen in Lake County become shorter so that access to the water is much easier by Harpersfield in Ashtabula County. Eventually the river looks like a trickle and seems to lose itself in marshes and a farmer's field way down past U.S. 332. We are not sure where we are anymore – what county is this? Colby shouts, "It would be better to try this in winter when the trees are bare." Maybe when I get back on the ground and am lying down, that will sound like a good idea. Tracing the route as closely as possible in a car and crossing all the bridges sounds more attractive right now (Appendix C). I would also like to walk out in that bean field to the river's origins.

We give up and on the way back north, Colby suggests this would be a great day to see Cleveland. I nod assent knowing how much he likes to fly and wants to share that with me. And maybe level flying will help. Ten minutes later, he shouts, "There must be some politician is town. Air traffic is closed unless you file a flight plan." I shout back, "Oh, right. It was in the newspaper that President Bush is in Kirtland Hills this weekend meeting with his supporters." Home to Concord Airpark we go, and I use up the rest of my film on photos of his plane and the hangar – even trying for an artistic shot of the wind sock. It feels good to walk on earth again.

When I get home, I look at an Ohio map. We had ended up somewhere south of Mosquito Reservoir, nowhere near the river's beginnings. I'm glad we did the plane trip even though I had to lie flat for 15 minutes to finally get rid of the airsickness. Besides seeing the magnificent Grand River sculpture and how it lies, we saw a half moon above one of the huge clouds momentarily and Little Mountain's dark green top. Little Mountain – 1227 feet above sea level – is the highest land in Lake County, which is indeed little for a mountain.

(It's not the highest summit in Lake County. The Knob Summit, which I assumed was just the highest point on Little Mountain, is counted as a separate summit 1240 feet above sea level. There are seven named summits in Lake County, the shortest only 643 feet above sea level. None of the summits are on the list of the top ten peaks in Ohio, which is certainly not a mountainous state, and that word is not being used. According to *Webster's New World Dictionary*, a mountain is an elevation of land that rises more or less abruptly and is larger than a hill. A summit is the topmost point of a hill or similar elevation; a peak is the highest of a number of high points, and a hill is a natural raised part of the earth's surface, often rounded and smaller than a mountain. Go figure.)

Whatever, the Little Mountain is our mountain and linked geologically to the creation of the Grand River by glacial forces. It will maintain a vigil over the Grand River and Lake Erie long after my sojourn here has ended.

13 CONSERVANCIES

Saturday, August 14, 8:30 a.m., 59° F.

This is not Florida. We had planned on being there by 7:30 p.m. yesterday but our flight was canceled after we arrived at the airport (Hurricane Charley). We are back home awaiting news of our rescheduled departure time. We are still going to have our family vacation trip with Colby's son Duff, his wife Julie, and grandson Chase at a condominium twelve feet from the Gulf of Mexico in Clearwater. At three-going-on-four years old, Chase has been carrying around a toy airplane in anticipation of his first jet trip. He's been up in our Cessna 172, but this plane will be bigger and faster.

Because of the delay I am able to go to the Grand River today. As I drive out my lane, rabbits scramble into the meadow's higher grasses. It's sunny, but cool lately. I am looking forward to Florida's heat.

At the bridge the river is gurgling over exposed rocks upstream. Bells ring atop the south bluff. I've known about the bell tower for years and am always entranced whenever I hear it. The tower is on the Walden II property, Lake County's only Nature Conservancy site. Its 120 acres were given to the Conservancy by James Storer of Storer Broadcasting Company fame, who purchased the land for his country home in 1967. His concern for rivers, open lands and fresh air compelled him to be part of a citizen's group which petitioned the Ohio Department of Natural Resources to designate this section of the Grand River wild instead of scenic. A September 8, 1974 interview in the *Lake County Telegraph* quotes him as saying, "Designating it scenic would have brought a lot more people and more roads into the area and this would not have been any good. Now it is mostly wild and undeveloped and that's how I like it." Thank you, Mr. Storer.

Neighbors say he still lives at Walden II during the summer but winters in Florida. His name is listed as one of the trustees of the Grand River Partners, a non-profit organization dedicated to preserving the river and its tributaries' quality by protecting watershed land. Neighbors also say he built the bell tower for his first wife, Ann Tipton Storer, who died in 1985. (Mr. Storer died February 21, 2012 at age 86.) I know that visiting Walden II is by invitation only so I call the Ohio Nature Conservancy office. I am directed to fill out a visit request form which will be passed along to the Walden II caretakers.

Purple and yellow wildflowers bloom along the river's banks. A few swallows harvest flying insects. All is calm which calms me. Earlier today I had been watching the hurricane's destruction on TV. There are rumors of deaths; sixty body bags have been ordered by a safety director on Florida's western edge. I am grateful that we are safe. Colby often remarks that living here in northeast Ohio is the best – no hurricanes, rarely any earthquakes and even rarer tornadoes. The worst we seem to have to endure or enjoy (depending on your mindset) is some spectacular thunder, lightning, and snowstorms.

I read about the greatest natural disaster in Ohio (so far) - the 1913 flood. On Friday, March 21, a sixty mph gale crossed the state from west to east blowing down a lot of buildings and trees. The rains started Sunday, March 23, dumping nine to eleven inches all over the Midwest, New England and upper southern states. The most severely hit area in Ohio was along the Great Miami River at Dayton. On Tuesday morning, two levees broke and the city was covered in twenty feet of water. The death toll in Ohio was variously listed as 428 or 467 people with 20,000 to 40,000 homes destroyed. The Ohio River crested at sixty-seven feet on March 31.

Lake County had one death. First the gale force winds blew over trolley poles on the C.P. & E. railroad east of Painesville; the passengers had to walk home. After the rains came, the Grand River rose over four and a half feet from 2:30 to 4:00 a.m. late Monday night, flooding all the flats along its course and removing three bridges in Painesville. Many people remained in their homes on the flats although water came in the first floor of their houses. Some needed rescuing by horse-drawn wagons or boats. *The Painesville Telegraph* reported hundreds of people gathered at the East Main Street dam to watch the twenty foot high rapids. It was rumored that the bridges at Vrooman and Blair roads were also gone, but both stood. The Blair Hollow Bridge (then so named) was described in the newspaper as "an historic one of the old-fashioned covered kind." It wasn't until Friday that the Grand River was back in its channel. The flood was called one of the worst but failed to reach the prior high water mark set in the 1893 flood. Oh, another flood to research.

After the 1913 flood waters receded, public demand for disaster prevention resulted in the 1914 passage of the Ohio Conservancy Law. The legislation gave Ohio's government the authority to establish watershed districts. Although challenged in both state and federal supreme courts, the law was upheld. In 1915, the Miami Conservancy District became the first watershed district in the nation.

Today at the Blair Road Bridge, the water level is low enough that some gravel beds are visible. I can see the bottommost layer of stones that holds back the soil and supports the bridge at its north end in this broad valley with a shallow river languorously flowing west. It's hard to imagine the amount of water that must have come through here in 1913 and washed away both approach ramps to the covered bridge. I wonder if that is when the original cut stones on the south embankment were replaced by concrete – more likely it was in 1952 when the covered bridge was torn down.

When I return home, I smell toast, sausage and tea. Chase is exclaiming over the frogs in Rana Pond. I telephone my parents at their central Ohio farm and reassure them we are still safe here in LeRoy Township, but will be leaving for Florida today. I must admit I am curious to see what happened there. No damage has been reported at Tampa Bay, our landing destination, and the weather station forecasts only mild winds.

We learn that our plane is leaving at 2 a.m. The regular flight routes go first before the catch-ups – which is us. It's going to be a long day. Naps might be wise – good luck with Chase – what can we do to wear him out? I did get my time with the river, though. And I'll be back next weekend to see it again.

Aerial view on August 7

14 SUBJECT TO FLOODING

Sunday, August 22, 6:30 p.m., 72° F.

We are back from Florida. Something happened at the bridge while I was gone. There's a pile of dirt just over the right guardrail as you approach from the south – close to where I park my car at the end of the Tudor house's driveway. Maybe the homeowners are planning to do some landscaping. I find it unsettling. I wasn't expecting change at my river.

The early evening sunlight strikes only half of the river in both directions, highlighting some trees while leaving others in dark. Downstream the waters are still and reflective of the shadowed trees except at the northwest bend where some trunks are backlit by sunshine. Upstream minuscule riffles are dancing in the sunlight. Gravel beds protrude from both banks. The air is warm but still. It is so pleasant gazing at all things beautiful.

I'm reading *Self-Portrait with Turtles* by David M. Carroll. Since the age of eight, he has loved turtles, but he keeps losing his observation sites when the turtles' habitats are destroyed by development or "progress" as some call it. I don't want that to happen to my Grand River. It surprises me how disturbing some dumped dirt is.

Fortunately, there are people dedicated to preserving the river. Grand River Partners, Inc. is a citizen-driven, non-profit land trust working to preserve the river, its tributaries, and watershed. Since 1994, it and other conservation organizations have permanently protected roughly 24,000 acres of the 455,680 watershed acres. It's great to look at their watershed map and see patches of purchased or protected lands (Appendix A). Most of the protected lands are by conservation easements which seek to eliminate development as a potential future land use. In return for a fee or tax benefit, the landowner retains ownership and certain rights – flexible enough to meet each individual's needs. These easements are permanent, recorded on the property's deed, and do not grant public access. What a great idea! My wish is that those red and yellow-coded map patches will become contiguous along the Grand River's banks.

Conservation easements, however, can't stop all change. Nature has a say too. In Florida, the effects of Hurricane Charley were pronounced at Punta Gorda about one hundred miles south of our Clearwater Beach vacation site. There was no damage where we were and the weather was perfect. In the late afternoon thunderheads would form inland, eventually displaying a lightning show, but it didn't rain on us. It seemed surreal vacationing as usual while nearby homeless residents were struggling for food, water, and shelter.

One day, we drove east across the state to Melbourne Beach on the Atlantic Ocean to visit Colby's aunt. On our way through Kissimmee, near Disney World, we saw hurricane damage – downed signs, uprooted trees, missing roof sections, electric outages – but the roads were clear. On our way back, we needed gas and searched several miles before finding an open service station where we joined a rapidly extending line of cars. Some cars were driving over the berm and tree lawn to jump the queue. Night had fallen; the side streets behind the station had no electricity; supplies we take for granted were scarce.

A tornado or flood could alter the Grand River, not to mention the effects of a severe earthquake. As bad as the 1913 flood was in all of Ohio, the 1893 flood caused more deaths in northeast Ohio. Fourteen people lost their lives to the floodwaters here and east into northwest Pennsylvania. Rain started on Monday, May 15, and didn't stop until Wednesday, May 17. All flood zones in Painesville were flooded. Water there filled the entire valley to its bluffs, establishing the current high-water mark. Newspaper accounts report that N.T. Breed on his milk wagon had just gotten across the Furnace Bridge when it was washed away. The Main Street Bridge, although damaged, held, but fifty feet of the east approach was destroyed. There is no mention of the Blair Road Bridge except a general statement that "Roads and culverts in all directions have been badly injured or washed out. Many bridges large and small have been weakened or carried away."

An exciting time was had by the Korth family who worked a farm below: "Vrooman's crossing on the Grand River...As the family was sitting down to dinner Wednesday noon a large area of land weighing many tons and carrying a number of large trees started from the top of the bluff, two hundred feet above the house, and descending with terrible force rushed into the river beneath, carrying everything before it. Fortunately the slide did not strike the house squarely. Only the edge came in contact but disastrous results followed. Without warning, the house was thrown into the air, turned over and fell heavily into the cellar. The household furniture, stoves, tables and chairs together with the members of the family were buried into a promiscuous heap. Miraculous as it seems, Mr. and Mrs. Korth and the children escaped with but few bruises. The house and household goods are wrecked and Mr. Korth lost all his tools and farming implements, which together with the outhouses were swept into the river. Mr. Korth has the sympathy of the community and a subscription has been started for his benefit."

By May 24, the local newspaper reported countywide damages at $50,000 and predict that refilling the lost Main Street Bridge approach will cost about $1000. One article said: "It is thought that the best economy demands the addition of another span to the Main Street Bridge for relief in times of flood. It is a well known fact that the river is subject to spring and fall freshets each year and that these are growing more severe as forests are cleared off and farms drained."

This ecological post-disaster discussion sounds like ones that occur today, only now it's global. The Main Street Bridge today is wider, but the road east still dips as it traverses the flood zone filled with condominiums, single homes, and businesses. I wonder what would happen there if another large flood occurs that equals or exceeds the 1893 one.

Except for the dirt pile, nothing seemingly has changed here at the Blair Road Bridge. Water still flows over the same gravel beds; insects and birds are active. And yet, much has changed. New wildflower blooms have appeared; old ones have dropped to the ground to decay and enrich the soil. Raccoons have come and eaten and bathed. Wild berries have been consumed. Maybe a coyote has sipped from the cool waters. I am older by seven days. To imagine I may have only 20 more years left on this earth is startling and saddening. The Grand River has only added a speck of time to its history. As Colby, my sage, says, "The earth could flick us humans off (like we flick a mosquito off our skin) and keep on going as if nothing had happened."

15 GRAND RIVER PARTNERS

March 18, 2009

I arrive at the Austin building on Lake Erie College in Painesville to meet with the staff of the Grand River Partners. Outside room 313, a large map of the Grand River and its watershed hangs on the wall (Appendix A). Inside the open door in a room approximately twelve by twenty feet are four people with desks, chairs, computers, and storage cabinets. Papers and books are piled on all flat surfaces including the floor; maps cover the walls. I am meeting with the acting director, an executive assistant, and two land protection specialists. They clear a chair for me and we talk about their organization that works at "Preserving the Grand – Leaving a Legacy."

Q – Where does the Grand River begin and what is its correct length? I've seen both 98.5 and 102.7 miles in print.

A – It begins on the Irwin farm north of Parkman in Geauga County. The length depends on how you measure it. Two unnamed tributaries merge to start the river, so if you assume one of the streams is the source you get the longer mileage. We start our count at the point they join.

Q – At what mile is the Blair Road Bridge? I've been trying to figure that out and have guessed it at mile 73.

A – The bridge is at mile 17.3 because river miles are traditionally counted from the mouth to the tail – opposite of the water's flow.

Q – Tell me about the origins of your organization.

A – James P. Storer, who is the board president now and established Walden II in LeRoy Township, was the primary instigator in forming the Grand River Partnership. It's a loose consortium of government and private groups who have an interest in the river. In 1994 it was decided that a private, non-profit, membership agency could best handle the work needed to preserve and protect the river water and now the Grand River Partners is one of the biggest such agencies in Ohio.

Q – Beside membership fees, where do you get your funding?

A – Private foundations, fundraising, donors, state and federal land protection grants – particularly Clean Ohio bonds which were just renewed.

Q – Was the Grand River the first Ohio river to be designated Wild and Scenic?

A – No, Little Beaver Creek was the first, getting its designation the night before the Grand River did. (The Wild River designation specifies that the river's banks are at least seventy-five percent forested to a depth of at least 300 feet. Ohio now has three thus labeled: Little Beaver Creek in Columbiana County, our Grand River and Conneaut Creek in Ashtabula County.)

Q – How many dams were there on the river and what has happened to them?

A – There were originally four, but only two remain. The ones on Mill Race in Geauga County and Mill Street in Painesville (Lake County) are gone. The fifteen foot high East Brook Dam in Parkman (Geauga County) was built in 1952. It is operated by the Great Western Reserve Council. The eight and a half foot tall Harpersfield Dam in Ashtabula County was built in 1913 primarily for flood control and is now under the auspices of the Ashtabula MetroParks. That dam is failing; water is getting into and around the bulkhead.

Q – Should it be repaired or removed?

A – It's hard to say. At present, the dam is preventing the migration of sea lampreys farther upstream. The U.S. Fish and Wildlife Service is trying to eradicate them by releasing TFM into the water; they did a treatment last fall. TFM has the least impact of all available chemicals, but it's also killing the salamanders and may terminate the mud puppies. Mud puppies take seven years to breed the next generation. If the river is treated every year, they don't have a chance. There is an alternative treatment being discussed – a pheromone locator. The other argument for not removing the dam is the effect of all the sediment now built up behind the barrier. But that shouldn't be a problem. The Grand River's seasonal flow surges will take care of the sediment. Of course, either path – removal or repair – will cost millions of dollars.

Q – What other nonnative species are in the waters?

A – First of all, there are no zebra mussels. They cannot tolerate the current. The nonnative fish are the goby, primarily in the lower end, the white perch and the steelhead trout, which do not seem to have any adverse effects.

Q – What groups are doing research on the Grand River?

A – Primarily it is the Ohio EPA, but the Cleveland Museum of Natural History owns some land along the river and focuses its surveys and research on rare species.

Q – What natural disasters have affected the Grand River?

A - Besides the rerouting of the mouth of the Grand River to Fairport Harbor after an earthquake way back before human habitation, there have been no changes from floods or earthquakes. The 2006 flood reshaped some tributaries, but did not change the course of the river itself (Chapter 59).

Q – Who uses water from the Grand River?

A – That was one of the original uses for the Harpersfield Dam, but not any longer. I'm not sure about the other dam (East Brook).

Q – Tell me about the land abatement program.

A – Currently 35,000 acres of land are protected by either conservation easements, direct ownership by us or any of the participants in the Grand River Partnership or land management stewardship. We own 3,000 acres. Initially, we took advantage of any opportunities that came our way, relying primarily on the willingness of volunteers. Now we consider ourselves a watershed conservation agency. Our overall goal is to protect the "right" twenty-five percent of the watershed lands. The U.S. Geological Survey urges protection of the most biologically diverse areas and those that impact the river's flow into Lake Erie. We started with a good river and we want to keep it that way. If unable to purchase or get an easement for critical lands, then we work to help the landowner protect the water. Most landowners want to do so since they were attracted there by the river.

Q – What are the greatest threats to your goal?

A – Insensitive development is one. We are not against development, but it is a race against time to get priority properties. Development is down seven percent in Lake County, but up twenty percent in Geauga County. We hope to persuade developers that there are benefits to not building at the river's edge – that wetlands and bank reinforcement with natural vegetation increases the value of the properties that are placed farther from the water. We are delighted when a developer comes to us first with questions about preserving the river. That developer realizes more money might be made if what attracts people in the first place is preserved.

Failing septic systems are a problem for the river and particularly for new owners who face upgrading costs. We'd like to see more inspections and upgrades. Implementation of environmental regulations lags in Trumbull and Ashtabula counties – Lake and Geauga counties do much better. Agriculture still contributes some problems, but that has improved. We have to educate the people who call complaining about the muddy and opaque nature of the Grand River in the lowlands. Muddy and messy is not pollution – that its nature there. Only when the river turns west in Ashtabula County does its water clear going through the gorges along the escarpment.

The EPA monitors the TMDL (total maximum daily load), giving a grade for the quality of the water based on what it can handle. So far, the Grand River has scored over 90 out of 100. To keep it that way, restoration, preservation, and protection are needed. A healthy river makes good economic sense for fishing, recreation, and human health.

It's important to be respectful of resources, to use the land in ways that conserve the river's quality. We'll join efforts with any organizations or individuals that are working on conservation of the Grand River.

Q – It looks like you could use more space. Wouldn't you like to have an office somewhere along the Grand River?

A – Yes, we are looking for a bigger office. But we wonder if being on the river might distract us from our work.

After an hour I leave with a large packet of brochures, a CD, a lapel button, and a sticker for my car. I am impressed by their passion, enthusiasm, and commitment – this is not just a job. I wish them more space in an office somewhere along the Grand River even if they would find the views distracting. It only makes poetic sense for them to enjoy seeing every workday what they strive to preserve.

NOTE: Before this book went to print, the economic downturn resulted in the layoff of two of the four staff members mentioned above; the board of trustees decided to join with the Western Reserve Land Conservancy as the Grand River chapter; the office was moved farther east to 70 South Park Place – only two blocks from the river. I hope an upturn sees all staff returned to the jobs they love. The Grand River needs them. You can help by becoming a Guardian of the Grand, a Stewart of Streams, a Conservator of Creeks, or an Observer of Otters by making a donation. I couldn't resist doing the Otter thing. (www.wrlandconservancy.org)

16 SHALE AND SILTSTONE

Thursday, September 2, 10:30 a.m., 70° F.

Somehow I have skipped a week. What have I been doing? I remember a few days of crossing the Blair Road Bridge when the mist rising from the water was spectacular, but I didn't have my camera with me. Maybe I should invest in another camera. Colby has reading glasses in cups in all rooms, garage and car. Redundancy equals readiness.

When I arrive at the bridge today, a workman with a caution sign directs me to the left side of the road. I see county road employees streaming steaming tar (I couldn't resist) on pavement cracks on the far side of the bridge. I still can reach my usual parking place on the right, so I pull in, turn my hazard lights on, shut off the engine, and leap out with my camera.

"Hello," the workman calls, seemingly ready to forestall my approach. Homeland Security on the Blair Road Bridge?

"I'm just taking pictures of the river," I respond, and go on to the spot where I place my camera on the concrete barrier. My next shot directly across the water includes the workers and their truck.

"You work for the *News-Herald*?" he calls.

"No, I just do this for myself. I take pictures every week and write about it," I say.

"Car coming," he volunteers as I cross the road to get the downstream photo.

The south bluff shadows the lazily-flowing river so that it looks like a black shiny ribbon next to the forest's deep green on the right bank. Only the treetops are sunlit – their leaves chartreuse. But the blue and white sky is reflected and brightens the water at the bridge. Upstream most of the north bank is sunlit. Are the workers aware and awed by the beauty around them as I am, or are they so focused on their task that they miss seeing the grandeur here? There is no wind. I can easily hear the workers talking, but can't make out their words. The air is hot tar pungent. Soon the asphalt cracks will be sealed and the valley will be left alone again except for passing traffic.

"Have a good day," I say over my shoulder as I get back into my car and leave him wondering about the woman who stopped to snap photos of the river. Just as I am writing about him now, maybe he shared a story about me when he went home that night. It seems I want to be noticed too.

Back at my house I continue research on the Grand River. The Ohio Department of Natural Resources has two web pages on the designated Wild and Scenic River (www.dnr.state.oh.us). The Grand

River lobe of the Wisconsinan glacier during the Pleistocene or Ice Age determined the snaky shape of the river. Its headwaters can be found in Portage and Geauga counties. There are two county sources? Contradictory information abounds on the river's headwaters. One would think this issue would be resolved by this time.

The real gold mine, however, is a book I bought, *The Ohio Nature Almanac*, with pages of geology information in understandable but sleep-inducing words. I'll do my best to paraphrase it for you. Ohio reached its current location 50 million years ago, plus or minus several million years, but the Ice Age commenced only about one million years ago. Out of Canada came four glaciers – the Nebraskan, Kansan, Illinoian, and Wisconinan. It was the last one that 40,000 years ago covered most of Ohio - only the southeast part of the state escaped. Moving at breakneck speeds of 160-220 feet per year, the glacier took 12,000 years to move over the land. The ice at its perimeter was 50-200 feet thick, but at the Ohio and Ontario border, the weight of mile high ice depressed the Earth's surface enough to give us Lake Erie when the ice melted about 12,000 years ago.

Piles of rocks, gravel, sand and clay were deposited directly by glaciers contributing to today's topography. Our current winds, running water, and ice still have some effect on the land, but oh-so-slowly and definitely less pronounced. Geologists have had their say; the Blair Road Bridge section of the Grand River is in the Grand River Low Plateau of the Glaciated Allegheny Plateau. As the river heads north to Lake Erie, it ends in the Huron Erie Lake Plains.

I like having these names to throw around in conversations – hopefully never in front of a geologist. Do they have any markers like dust around their nostrils or pebbles rattling in their pockets so I can identify them before making a fool of myself?

Speaking of rocks, the banks and bed of the Grand River are primarily Chagrin Shale. And wait until you hear the names of the top soil types in the Grand River Watershed: Sheffield silt loam, Mahoning silt loam, Holly silt loam, Platea silt loam, Remsen silt loam, Darien silt loam, Canadice silt loam, and, my favorite, Caneadea-Candice complex. The last one would make a good mental illness diagnosis.

"What's the matter with you? You can't run dog sleds down the Grand River. And why is your hair so sticky?

"I can't help myself. The doctor said I have this Caneadea-Candice Complex."

"Well, get over it before someone writes about you. This family has been through enough, and we are not going to Canada again this weekend. What in the world is so interesting about Canada anyway?"

There's another prehistoric rock at the river – siltstone. Harder than shale and resistant to weather, you see its layers peeking out of the high shale bluffs, exposed in horizontal lines like a giant piece of baklava. Both types of rocks were formed during the Devonian Period, the Age of Fishes. How appropriate. As *The Ohio Nature Almanac* states: "A view of the river in this area is truly spectacular especially following spring and summer showers when waterfalls cascade over the steep shale bluffs." Something to look forward to after the coming winter.

I look up the definitions for bank, bluff, cliff, gorge and valley. I just never would have called any portion of the Grand River a gorge based on what I have seen elsewhere in the United States. Here it is: a bank is a stretch of rising land at the edge of a body of water, a bluff is high, steep land with a broad flat front, while a cliff is steep and broad but primarily rock. A gorge is a deep and narrow pass between steep heights (how is narrow defined?) and a valley is the lowland between hills (oh, dear) with a river running through it. So the Grand River has valleys, banks, bluffs, and possibly gorges – Ohio gorges, that is.

Now I am curious about how high the shale walls (bluffs) are here at the bridge. I am guessing they rise at least 200 feet. I wonder if I can use my walking cane that is labeled in hand measurements for determining the height of horses. It came with instructions on how to figure tree heights, but that requires pacing a certain distance from the object being measured which might put me in the river. Something to schedule before the fall rains come.

17 WATERCOURSES

Thursday, September 13, 10:15 a.m., 70° F.

On my way to work I am just past the spot where I park for my Grand River forays when I remember today's the best day to gaze at the Grand River and get my weekly photos. And I don't want to miss stopping because two inches of rain fell recently, courtesy of the last hurrah of Hurricane Francis. I brake and back up to park at the end of the Tudor house driveway. That's when I am caught.

Slender Man and Slender Woman, who look middle-aged, are standing in the driveway next to their house. I notice their slender physiques because I am struggling to remove the extra 25 pounds I have added to my ectomorphic frame since age 50. I'd like to blame my thyroid disease, and can somewhat according to the doctor, but mostly I've been eating more and exercising less. I do, however, blame both my left knee that swells and hurts with any activity (I'm debating surgery) and my fine cook of a husband.

Confident that my car is not in their way, I jump out and rush to the bridge. The river is swollen just past its banks with cinnamon-colored water. The tree trunk debris usually seen on the right eastern bank is covered by water or may have traveled all the way to Painesville for all I can tell. The blue sky above heralds a lovely late summer day. The rain has stopped – only the river bears witness to the volume of moisture released in this locale over the past three days.

At home I keep track of rainfall with the largest rain gauge I could find. It will need to be emptied before algae starts to grow in the two inches of water in the transparent plastic tubing with its large yellow numbers and lines that I can see from inside my house. The funnel cup on top has faded to a mellow green. I look forward each spring to hanging that cheap piece of plastic in its place on the top of the deck post. And in early winter I wait until the first snow fills the hollow tube before storing it, cleaned and dried, in the garage. It's a ritual that connects me to the weather and nature just like stopping at the Grand River is doing.

Earthwatch, which appears weekly in our newspaper, does the same connecting worldwide. Its synopsis of storms, plagues, earthquakes, and animal phenomena is highlighted by related symbols on a global map. I like having this bigger picture to keep my daily minutiae in perspective.

After I cross the road and take my final picture, Slender Woman drives by and smiles in my direction. Evidently my behavior is not a cause for alarm. Are there other people stopping at the end of her driveway to photograph the river? Maybe she and Slender Man were looking at me through binoculars when I sat across the river for an hour a few weeks ago taking some telescopic photos of their house. I had my Advantix camera for several years before my brother-in-law pointed out that it had a 30-60 mm zoom which I now use at the drop of a hat. Another camera feature, however, drives me crazy. One can select normal, classic or panoramic pictures - once I inadvertently got large views of Colby's head.

I return to my car. Slender Man is still standing in his driveway looking my direction. I wave, but don't wait for a response; I don't want to be late to work. As I drive over the bridge I look again at the brown water rushing under the bridge only to bump up against the south bluff before curving northwest. Streaming down the face of the Chagrin shale/siltstone bluff are several flows of water that appear only after or during rainstorms. Yes, they are falls of water, but not true waterfalls, which I assume are constant.

I go for my dictionary when I get back home after work. I think they are freshets – a rush of water or sudden overflowing because of heavy rain or melting snow. After following the trail for watercourses through the pages of *Webster's New World Dictionary*, the order from largest to smallest is probably such: river, stream, creek, brook (synonymous with rivulet, streamlet, runnel and burn), then rill or brooklet, and a trickle. I can't figure out where to put a freshet in that listing since they are sporadic, and some of the other categories also depend on rainfall for their existence. If you want to go the other way, watercourses run into pools, ponds, lakes, and seas before mixing with the oceans. The recent storms produced freshets at the Grand River that swell its volume as it rushes downstream to Lake Erie, eventually joining the Niagara River which flows into Lake Ontario and on to the St. Lawrence Seaway before emptying into the Atlantic Ocean. I see the whole route in my mind, even swirls in the ocean.

18 SKUNKS AND RATTLESNAKES

Thursday, September 23, 8 a.m., 65° F.

I think I am a set of photos behind my essay - maybe not - I'll know when I get them developed. Once before I had a set of photos and no writing to go with it. You would think this project would be easy to keep track of; at least it seemed that way when I started.

Yesterday at 7:45 a.m. on my way to Ashtabula, there was a dense mist filling the Grand River valley up to the bottom of the high, long bridge on State Route 528. These bluffs are at least 200 feet higher than those at the Blair Road Bridge. Autumn sunlight crowned the postcard-perfect scene.

At work, the health care clinic was inspected by the feds. They didn't like our chart folders – papers could fall out. Clasp ones will cost more money and I predict that within ten years electronic records will be required. I found it unsettling to be told to see more low income clients while spending limited funds on paper. I'm so glad the Grand River is nearby. I need it.

Today I drive to the Blair Road Bridge as soon as I awaken at 8 a.m., my earliest time yet by nine minutes. A blue-hued mist is barely visible in the powerful fall light striking the bluffs. I wonder what it was like earlier this morning. I breathe deeply and gaze at the flowing water longer than usual. The river is full, its blue hue intensified by the shade that obscures any river bottom rocks. More mist can be seen high up in the western trees as the river goes out of sight. Some trees' leaves are showing fall colors, and a few branches are bare.

I think of Marietta, which was almost drowned by the Ohio River this week, thanks to Hurricane Ivan. And more rain and flooding may be coming. Instead of dissipating, the hurricane has looped back to the south and gathered more strength - another storm watch is on. The Ohio River is nine feet above flood stage. Would a nine foot rise in the Grand River here reach the Tudor house?

Things at work will get better or worse, but the river is still here and won't even notice when I am gone. Will I regret what I don't get done at work on my deathbed? I know I won't regret any time I have spent outdoors. Although I loved Paris and would like to visit again, I don't recall it as often as I do our Serengeti Plains' safari or Grand Canyon rafting trips. I won't regret any stop I make at the Blair Road Bridge either. It's a mini-vacation every week.

As I am writing back at the house, not only do I see Emmett perched on the deck chair outside my open window, I smell him. Skunk aroma rises from his fur like smoke from a pot of burning food and there is no tomato juice in the house. I leave a phone message for Mr. Whipple; the one everyone calls to trap unwelcome wildlife visitors. He probably knows how to remove skunk odors. Now Emmett is scraping the window screen. I e-mail a friend in Virginia who once worked as a veterinarian's assistant and may just know the magic potion that will free Emmett's fur from its noxious odor and allow him inside before nightfall. Who will save my cat from spending the night outside?

Of the 45 mammals found within the Grand River watershed, I wonder how many and which ones come to drink at the Blair Road Bridge. I would love to see a white-tailed deer lapping the water, a mink or red fox coming through the grasses, or a river otter (reintroduced in 1986) sliding down the bank. How about a flying squirrel leaping from black willow to black walnut to eastern cottonwood trees, the dominant floodplain species. Even a skunk with its striking black and white apparel would be welcome as long as it doesn't see me. And then there is the endangered Eastern massasauga rattlesnake. A Chippewa word meaning great river-mouth, the massasauga is the smallest of North America's rattlesnakes, reaching only thirty inches in length – that seems long enough. During the day, it stays in rodent burrows. At night it goes out to find and eat those rodents or frogs and lizards. Currently, this rattlesnake is only found in the Grand River lowlands. No one has seen it in the gorge section for over fifty years.

Maybe a nighttime sit with night-vision goggles is in order. Who has night-vision goggles? And do I dare to do this by myself now that I have learned that at least one, maybe three, black bears live in the township? I can think of a dozen excuses, particularly time.

Another scraping occurs at the screen accompanied by plaintive meows – it's going to be a long day. Maybe I will try my citrus deodorant spray. Colby complains that it's too potent, but potent is what I need. I'm off to traumatize the cat. Flow on, Grand River, where one or more skunks' sprays wouldn't be a big deal.

19 BUCKET LIST AND THE BEAR

Thursday, October 1, 10:25 a.m., 65° F.

I miss the mist again at the Blair Road Bridge. Yesterday on my way to Ashtabula, there was the most mist I've ever seen rising from the river at the State Route 528 Bridge. The top of the valley was clear but the whole floor was obscured by the fog, although even without the fog, you can't see the river from this bridge. The bottom is so deep and treed that no water is visible as you zoom by at 60 miles per hour high above.

At my bridge, everything is clear. The water has receded enough that rocks and rearranged gravel bars are visible. The bank grass is matted from the last overflow. A new shallow pool has formed near the path out to the road. But both old trunks remain – the one I use as a back rest and the other one across the river angled upstream.

Tree leaves are starting to fall in the woods, a few collecting on the river's banks. None are on the water itself where today's strong current would sweep them downstream. The air is cool, but the sun warms my back as I snap my photos. Yellow, gold, and red colors spotlight the views around me. How I wish to stay here instead of going on to work – another hour by the water is what I need.

Work is very busy. I know I'm stressed when I feel annoyed because a patient doesn't position herself correctly on the exam table even though she's had this exam annually for the past twelve years. I share my feelings with a co-worker and we share a small ain't-it-the-way laugh. All day long I talk to people. No wonder I love the river language even if it is roaring.

I dislike loud vehicle and machinery noises, especially freeway din. Rock concerts make my ears ring and my head hurt although I like the sensation of being lost in the music. Grandstands full of sports fans are tolerable if you are not sitting next to a screamer. And I often find parties fatiguing. Give me the roars of the northwest wind as it crochets the forest's treetops, orchestral thunder approaching from Lake Erie, a blizzard split by my house corners, and a downpour drumming on my roof.

It's time to plot my retirement again. In the fall of 2000, I made a list of 100 things I yet want to do. Since that time, I have accomplished 16 of them such as visiting Africa, paying off the mortgage, growing a redwood tree and adding more windows to my house. The most recent one I checked off was seeing a bear in the wild. It's time to tell you about our visit from the Hell Hollow bear. After reading on, you will understand why I look for bear when I visit the Blair Road Bridge.

It was around 11 p.m. on May 7. As we return home down our

lane, I gasp when the car lights swing past the bird feeders in our backyard.

"Colby, there's a bear!" I yell.

"Huh?" he replies.

"Stop, stop, there's a bear at the bird feeders."

He stops the car, its lights shining off the bear's eyes. We sit in shock and awe, whispering about its size, fur, nose, and claws, while the bear rolls one of our bird feeders on the gravel path. It's trying to get at the seeds, and although aware of us, seems to have no interest in us.

We decide to get out of the car but leave its lights on to spotlight the sight. We go in the front door, and thirty-two feet later are at the back door, only twenty-five feet now from the bear. Quietly opening the back door we go outside on our deck. I cannot believe we are outside with a bear, watching its actions as it occasionally glances our way. It finally gets to the birdseed by tearing apart the feeder with its paws.

"We don't want it getting used to humans or thinking our place has food. We should scare it away."

I get a cooking pot and wooden spoon. Colby does the banging, slowly approaching the bear on the brick walk that leads to the bird feeders and wood. The bear flees, then stops about twenty feet into the trees.

"Do it again," I call, "it's still out there."

This time the bear goes out-of-sight. We hear it crashing through fallen limbs and then no more. We decide not to tell anyone (except our neighbors to the north, whose barn doors are open with feed bags stacked next to horses and cattle in stalls). We don't want some shortsighted Neanderthal who hears about the bear coming out here, hoping to add a bear trophy to his den wall.

Colby leaves on a business trip in the morning. I hear noises that night and discover the following morning that something has wrenched my plastic composter apart. Its lid and access door are bent, and clumps of eggshells, potato peelings, and lovely black mulch are scattered on the ground.

When I arrive at work the next day, everyone is talking about the bear. Someone from our township had videotaped the bear at his bird feeders. The bear made a star appearance on the 11 o'clock TV news. So the word was already out. And that's my bear story.

Number eight on my to-do list is retiring. Colby may retire next April – his latest plan. I've got about five more years although I am determined never to work fulltime again. I love my four-day workweek. But I shouldn't wait on retirement to work on more of my goals and pleasures. I'm adept at doing lots of work in small increments at my job.

Why not apply that skill now instead of waiting for a bigger block of time. I want to walk my property paths with a cup of tea and gaze at everything at least once a week. I want to leave five minutes earlier for work and stay longer at the Grand River.

Meanwhile I check on the growth of the two sequoia trees we planted in the front lawn. Growing a giant sequoia tree was also on my list. It is possible to grow one in Ohio although it will take a lot longer for it to reach any substantial heights. One of mine, nicely green, has doubled in size but the other one's lower branches are brown. Just beyond each of them, I see matted grass circles under the serviceberries. Do deer sleep here? I have a motion sensor camera. Maybe this is where I place it, although I could sneak it onto a tree at the Blair Road Bridge.

Of course, writing a book is also one of the items on my list. How fortunate I am to live close by a river – a river that by its grandeur and fluctuation is so easy to love. But then I've never met a body of water that I didn't instantly love, including the puddles that form on my driveway or the backyard swale that fills and flows after rainstorms or snowmelts.

20 AUTOPILOT

Thursday, October 7, 8:21 a.m., 58° F.

I'm three miles away from home when I realize I don't have my camera again. I have to get my photos today because my husband and I are going away this weekend. His Merchant Marine classmates are having a reunion at the Sawmill Creek Resort in Huron, west of Cleveland along the Lake Erie shoreline. I've always wanted to go there. The 465 acres of the Sheldon Marsh State Nature Preserve are just west of the resort's parking lot. *Birder's Digest* reports the preserve is a great birding spot and offers unspoiled views of Lake Erie from its beach.

On my way back to the house to get my camera, I chase two crows off the road. What are they eating? Farther down the road a dead bird lies on the center line. What kind of bird? Hitting the garage door opener halfway down the driveway, I rush through the open door. My camera is not at its usual storage spot – an antique child-sized, rolltop desk that also holds phone and address books, pens and pencils, and the answering machine. The camera is not on the dining room table, the piano, the mudroom mirror shelf. Oh, my, I bet it's in the car after all. Yes, there it is in the cubbyhole where I put it. I hope I won't be late to work now.

Back down the road I hurry. There's not time to stop and identify the dead bird. Farther on where there were two crows, there are now four crows fleeing my car's approach. There's no road kill here. Are they just meeting for a morning conversation, this quarrel of crows? How black their feathers are. They silently fly off – two west and two east.

At the river, my routine is automatic. I pull off the road, shove the gearshift into park, turn off the engine, crank on the emergency brake since I'm still on the hill, push the hazard button, grab my camera, and look at the door lock to make sure I don't accidentally push it before closing the door. No sight or sound of any cars. The river waits.

The water volume seems lower than anytime since I began my visits. The downed tree trunk on the east bank is completely out of the water with a large gravel bed visible in front of it. Although it's cool, the sun is out, but it illuminates only the top half of the trees climbing the bluff on the upstream bend. No sunshine reaches the river's black waters, but sky reflected there is bluer than the sky above.

The shortening days are noticeable. Soon I may not be able to take photos before my 8:30 a.m. workday starting time. I have one shot left after taking the usual three photos, so I do one more on the bridge itself using its railing to frame the view. If this turns out to be a better photo, I may rethink my routine – no, it's too late for that – I'll stay true to my original plan.

Isn't that the way it goes? Always some new thought or scrap of knowledge changing everything. Even though I know the only thing certain in life is change, I long for moments of sameness. I mistakenly think the Grand River is a constant in my life when it changes everyday. But it would take a fast trip through time's geological ages to see the differences. The water is up, down, over the banks, dried up, frozen, flooding, carrying debris. I'm looking forward to flipping through my weekly photos when this year long project is completed.

I'm wearing a jacket for the first time this fall. It slows down my arm movements, but the collar snuggled against my neck feels nice. There's no breeze, just a morning's coolness across my cheeks. I wish there was time to go to the Grand River's edge and stick my fingers in the unhurried water.

I am discovering that there are lots of people who come to survey, study, research, or manage the Grand River: Environmental Protection Agency, Ohio Department of Natural Resources, U.S. Geological Society, U.S. Army Corps of Engineers, U.S. Fish and Wildlife Service, The Nature Conservancy, Holden Arboretum, and the Cleveland Museum of Natural History. When I check out only the Cleveland Museum of Natural History's website, there are 95 pages that mention the Grand River. Within those pages are research projects (the four-toed salamander comes up often), studies of river otters, bobcats, and bird life (screech owl is mentioned more than once), flood plain details, offerings for outings, and volunteer clean-up opportunities. With all that going on, it's a wonder I don't see more people at the Blair Road Bridge. It's good to read that the Cleveland Museum has purchased 3,600 wetland acres in northern Ohio for preservation. The lands they are interested in have at least one unique natural community. I'm grateful for them, and the moments I carve out of my busy life to gaze upon the waters of the Grand River at one locale.

21 WINE REGION

Thursday, October 14, 8:12 a.m., 46° F.

Cooler weather coupled with shortening daylight makes it definitely feel like fall. I'm trying just one more set of photos in the early morning light on my way to work – the light may have already reached its full intensity on this cloudy October day. The river's water level continues low – no rain recently, but it should be coming soon from the collecting clouds. I'm disappointed by the tree colors at the river's edge. There are only a few bright yellows and reds in the valley although the sumac on the southeast bank is blood red. At home upon the plateau, more of the leaves are brilliantly colored - perhaps different temperature gradients have something to do with it.

The Grand River valley is a designated wine region - like Napa in California and Provence in France. The Winegrowers of the Grand River Valley lists five wineries within a ten mile span. One of them, St. Joseph's Vineyards in Madison, is only six miles from my house. I first met Art and Doreen, the vintners, when I impulsively knocked on their door one fall night on my way home from the Ashtabula clinic. The Sunday before my knock-knock-knock, I had read in *The Plain Dealer* that St. Joseph's Pinot Noir Reserve won first place at the International Riverside Wine Competition in California. That got my attention because Colby has often stated that there are no good red Ohio wines. So when I showed up at Art and Doreen's door requesting a bottle of their prize-winning Pinot Noir and related Colby's comment, I was escorted to the tasting shed and treated to a sampling of all their varietals.

Leaving thirty minutes later – or was it forty minutes – with my bottle of Pinot Noir Reserve, I drove carefully home. Colby was sitting at the dining room table reading his mail.

"Here," I said. "Open this bottle."

He did, we drank, he conceded he was wrong about red Ohio wines, and the rest is history. At a later visit to St. Joseph's, Art explained why this is a wine region and now we pester him to repeat his talk whenever we show up with uninitiated guests.

It all goes back to the four glaciers which carved out the Great Lakes and deposited a ridge of fertile soil ideal for the cultivation of vineyards. Lake Erie's large body of water, which holds heat in the fall and cold longer in the spring, reduces the threat of frost in the spring and extends the growing season in the fall so the grapes have time to ripen. As the air cools on a fall evening, colder air rushes down the Grand River valley to the flood zone in Painesville. Around 3 a.m., warmer air comes back up keeping the grapes warmer longer in the fall. The gentle slopes, where the vines are planted, carry away rainwater from the vines' roots. This perfect combination of extra warmth and adequate drainage promotes more concentrated sugar and flavor in the grapes.

One of the smallest wine regions in the world, the Grand River region is ideal for making ice wine, that super-sweet dessert wine concocted from frozen grapes after the temperature has dropped below twenty-one degrees for three consecutive nights. Art and Doreen go out in the middle of the night to pick these jewels each year the weather cooperates. It's a gamble but well worth the risk. I have volunteered to be called in the middle of the night when the harvesting needs to be done, but so far no phone call. Maybe they don't believe I mean it. I also want to go over some fall night and be there to experience the rise in temperature at 3 a.m. I think one would experience the same effect at the Blair Road Bridge. Three in the morning? Well, I'll think about it.

22 FOG AND HAWK

Tuesday, October 19, 8:08 a.m., 51° F.

As I leave my house, I enter the fog – a wonderful blanket of gray making it seem like I need to put a fresh contact lens in each eye. Maybe today I photograph the Grand River appearing out of a mist. I pass a school bus and am reminded of waiting at the side of the road with my brother and sister for our school bus to emerge from a fog. I loved the mystery of it all, feeling dampness on my face and hair while wondering what would appear next out of the gray curtain before being saved by the large yellow bus.

At the river today, the air is almost clear. Only a haze is visible over the water which becomes a little thicker up the valley walls. I take my dull pictures – no sun, no mist, no rain – although there was a rainstorm yesterday and more water is flowing again, not that it will be apparent in the photos. The river is dark but tree reflections can be seen.

I'm still not impressed by the bronze and brown leaf colors here. Only as I climb out of the river valley do I see red, yellow and orange leaves, brilliant even on this dull day. Maybe the flood zone just lags behind in its changes. Hopefully, winds won't remove the leaves until they put on a show by the water.

I drive on to the Painesville city limits, slowing down to view the river valley south of Madison Avenue. The fog clings to the treetops here, looking like a gossamer bedspread. And there's a hawk on a utility wire eyeing the road's grass berm. I stop as far off the road as I can get and methodically memorize the bird's markings. The beak is black with a touch of yellow above its nostrils, the chest is streaked and stippled with orange colors, the wings are mottled brown, the tail feathers have squared ends, and its feet and legs are yellow. I'm able to stay about three minutes, thrilled to be so close to a wild denizen of the air.

Back home eight hours later after work, I consult *Birds of North American* by Fred J. Alsop III, the complete guide to more than 930 species. My best guess is that the hawk was a juvenile broad-wing. This species makes up the bulk of hawk flights in September in the East (yes, it is October). It likes to watch for prey from utility poles and wires (yes, again) or near water along the edge of woods. Maybe I will see it later at the Blair Road Bridge. I also read that this hawk is protected by law. That's nice to know since large numbers were once shot during migration, particularly along mountainous ridges in the East. Protected means that the bird cannot be collected or held in captivity without a legal permit, and there is no hunting season for it.

So, I won't swear it was a broad-winged hawk, having been

wrong many times before when trying to identify birds. I may be wrong about the bird, but the encounter was totally mine. In addition to looking forward to seeing the Grand River several times a week as I cross it to and from work or stop for my visits, I'll be scouting more religiously for birds on wires. The Grand River Partners reports that 115 bird species have been identified in the watershed. I need more time by the river.

23 SECOND HOUR SIT

Tuesday, October 25, 11 a.m., 54° F.

The Walden II bells welcome me by chiming the hour. I plan to spend an hour again by the river and now I will know when my time is up – the bells will ring 12 times.

The air is cool, but the strong fall sun is warming. I walk to my downed tree seat, disturbing a fisherman in a red plaid shirt, red hat and knee-high waders. He moves farther upstream, just barely visible around the root ball of my seat. I brought with me a cup of tea with milk, my camera and binoculars, a wristwatch (which now I won't need), a tape measure and my notebook with pen.

The river runs full. The grass between my seat and the channel is bent flat from the higher water a few days ago after two inches of rain. The noonday sun above the south rim is so bright on the water that I cannot look directly at the Class I rapid to my right. Its rushing ripples help mute traffic passing on the bridge. I do lift my eyes at one vehicle's familiar sound. A school bus crawls across the bridge, braking at the south end to make the sharp turn before lumbering up the hill. Its yellow metal is perfect against the fall colors on the valley walls.

My view from my log seat includes the white trunks of sycamore trees highlighted by the sunlight, a far-off crow cawing as it flies, fast-flowing tannin-colored water that you can see into for at least two feet, another log across the river that has always been there (but now a bank of soil almost covers its trunk upstream) and graffiti.

Graffiti? I am stunned. On the lower half of the south concrete wall support under the bridge, someone has spray painted large black symbols. I look away and back several times to be sure that it's there. Graffiti? I don't know what it says or means. It doesn't matter – it is ugly in this wonderful view.

I have been taking photos since I arrived and have one exposure left. I walk down to the bridge, get as close as I can to capture this travesty on film. I want justice. I want the vandal to be caught and forced to canoe down the river with me from Harpersfield to Mason's Landing before cleaning up the graffiti. I want him/her to see and feel how jarring and disrespectful it is to desecrate the Grand River's beauty.

Young people (my assumption) with urges to leave their marks on the world cheapen the viewing pleasure for all. Why couldn't this perpetrator be satisfied with the railroad trestle's cement foot on Walnut Street in Painesville? The city tolerates graffiti there, only repainting it annually just in time for new writings of names, proclamations and Class of (put year here) when high school commencements near. Students consider graffitting the cement block a vaunted tradition. Even the railroad bridge high above has messages on it. I know who did the one that says, "I still love you, Jen" (with a backwards J), signed DFD. Fortunately, he didn't tell Colby, his father, until years later; the risks he took were great. I'd prefer not to see graffiti anywhere but accept that allowing it somewhere may keep it off other places. I suspect that's the theory or have the officials just given up?

Returning to my log seat, I choose not to let the graffiti ruin the rest of my experience – I will report it as soon as I leave the river. I focus on the three spiders that land on my clothing. The trees have lost fifty percent of their leaves A slight breeze loosens dozens of them, and one by one they softly plop on my head, my back, or the leaf litter already underfoot. A few make it to the river and ride the currents downstream. As I watch leaves floating on the water blued by the sky's reflection, I vow again not to look at the graffiti or my watch until the bell tower chimes twelve times.

There are five white pines around the houses on the south side. These have been planted since eastern hemlock is the native evergreen on hillsides here except for the top of Little Mountain, which has a different microclimate. The deciduous tree leaves are deep yellow, orange, red, rust, brown, magenta, and green – the full spectrum of fall colors at last. Two oaks less than thirty feet tall on the far side of the river still have green leaves with just a hint of yellow at their scalloped edges. A buzzard floats overhead. I take my jacket off; the sun is hot.

Looking past an arching sycamore branch far left, stretched out over the water in its quest for light, I scan the river as it makes an oxbow curve around a broad forested flatland. If I walked straight across the water and the land ahead for about 500 feet, I would meet the river again. I step to the river's edge and slip my tape measure in. The current pulls at the metal, but I estimate the water is three feet deep. I'm not crossing the river today – one would need hip boots and the water is cold. The fisherman is nowhere to be seen.

Faintly I hear the prelude and then 12 chimes, muffled by the river's downstream gurgling beyond the bridge. I look one more time at the graffiti and again feel sad. I decide to walk upstream from my log and see if I get back to my car as the fisherman may have done. I still think there is a trail or path next to the north valley wall. His truck was parked in the same pull-off as my car at the base of that bluff.

Walking next to the water is easiest; there's a worn path from animals and humans along the edge. I see deer tracks, piles of debris deposited from the last high water, a lone yellow daisy with a faint green center, ground cover with pink flowers that I think is purslane, and a duck box ten feet up a trunk. I wonder who put it there.

There it is – a trail leading up the bank into the trees. Off I go. Inside the woods, the understory is sparse. I meander under the canopy on and off any worn spot that looks like a trail and doesn't lead toward the brambles on my left. I'm glad I brought a tape measure, because there are some big trunks here.

The first tree I measure is a sycamore, ninety-eight inches in circumference four feet off the ground and leaning at a forty-five degree angle toward the east. Next I see a large maple tree that divides into four large trunks just two feet above the ground. Its circumference is sixteen feet. Another maple measures over sixteen feet, but any accuracy is gone when I realize that I am touching poison ivy vines and leaves. I vigorously wipe my hands on my pants. I hope I can make it home to wash the oils off my skin within the ten minutes deadline to prevent a reaction. Oh, my, do I have stories about prior encounters with the noxious weed.

It's too late to worry about that now. And here's another great tree, twenty-one feet around as I measure the air over its bark. I am alone with giants dropping their leaf gifts to the forest floor. I cannot hear the river but the bells announce the half-hour. It's 12.30 p.m. and I'm still making my way to the car. I know I am closer because the bells are louder. A brown maple leaf hits the top of my head. It measures seven inches wide and six inches long.

Moving closer to the steep north wall, I spy a dented, weathered, galvanized bucket and can't resist packing it along with me. It will make a great planter back home and I will have removed litter from the woods. I pass on the rusted water heater and a large tub, probably tossed over the rim above years ago. I'm not salvaging them; the earth will have to work its magic over time.

Too bad I am out of film. Here is an oak tree living parallel to the ground a foot off the soil. There's a slight arch in the middle of its fifty foot length that's rises to two feet. Seventeen branches, six to twenty feet tall, grow vertically from the horizontal trunk before it bifurcates into two smaller limbs. It's a cathedral – this would be a great place for sitting, but I move on. I notice pop cans, water bottles, gallon plastic containers, all within the last fifty feet to my car. I'm thinking teenagers did the graffiti, but this litter was probably left by adults. I don't get it. What's so hard about carrying out what you brought in? I would think people who love the river and its fish would be more responsible. I pick up and carry as much as I can to throw into my car's trunk.

There's a gigantic sycamore tree just across the road from my parked car that I have admired for sixteen years. Since I have a tape measure, it's a perfect time to get up close and personal. I straddle the guardrail, then stumble and slide on the slick, muddy embankment to the tree's base, where I discover that it's hollow. There's a two by three foot opening on the north side that a bear could use to get out of inclement weather. I'm glad I'm here. This tree may not last many more seasons. I set about measuring it. The trunk just above the soil is twenty-one feet around. Four feet up, three main branches start, two of them twelve feet in circumference and one eighteen feet. Sunlight strikes the mottled green, gray, and white trunks on the northeast sides, making the view upward breathtaking. I need more film.

Jumping into my car, I rush the three and one-half miles home, wash my hands and forearms that were exposed to the poison ivy leaves and sap (what will be will be) and grab a roll of film. When I get back to the tree, I expend all twenty-five exposures.

The sycamore, also known as a plane tree (*Platanus occidentalis*), is the largest living thing in Ohio – the biggest one ever recorded in Ashland County. It is the second largest broadleaf tree in the country and the largest flowering plant in North America. Known for its huge trunk hollows (so nothing is wrong with this one, it's just doing what it does), the trees used to be stuffed with youngsters going for packing records before phone booths and VW Beetles were available. I want a sycamore in my front yard.

There's a couple carrying their canoe to the river's edge down by the bridge. When they climb back into their truck and head in my direction, probably to park in the pull-off here, I flag them to a stop. The gentleman listens to my story of outrage over the graffiti under the bridge – which they will see as soon as their canoe hits the water – and agrees to also phone in a complaint.

Home I go. After taking a quick shower and shoving all my clothes in the washer, I start my phone calls. The Lake County Sheriff's office will send an officer right out to investigate. The Lake County Engineer's receptionist will let the Engineer know. The *News-Herald* desk staff agrees graffiti is unwelcome and will see if a reporter will do a story. I assure her the weather is perfect for some great pictures. The man answering the phone at Grand River Partners is most sympathetic and agrees that graffiti should be removed immediately to avoid copycats. He used to work for the parks' system, and that was their practice. He said he would contact the Ohio Department of Transportation. The woman at the LeRoy Trustee's office said the bridge was the responsibility of the Engineer's office.

"I understand, but please tell the trustees. Surely they will want to know that graffiti has appeared in our township," I say.

I'm giving all those named above one week before contacting them again if the graffiti is still there under the Blair Road Bridge. I will not accept this desecration of the Grand River.

24 THE COMING COLD

Monday, November 1, 8:04 a.m., 54° F.

The leaves are off most of the trees now at the Grand River, but the graffiti is still under the bridge. I suspect that removing graffiti is not at the top of the responsible agency's list since Election Day is tomorrow. The Lake County engineer position is up for grabs.

Today the cloudy sky dulls the landscape, but color persists in some of the tawny shrubs and green grasses along the river. On the north bank rim, evergreen eastern hemlock trees stand as sentinels among the barren deciduous trees. The river looks sometimes black, sometimes deep blue, as it streams gently past the land. The water level remains low. Soon more rain will come followed by snow. Soon I will need my silk underwear, thermal socks, and heavy jacket. I am relieved to report that I didn't get a rash after my exposure last week to poison ivy vines.

Election Day should be interesting – record crowds are predicted – hopefully lots of young adults and minorities will vote. I'm enjoying the computer-generated phone calls. I've heard from Bill Clinton and John Kerry while my daughter has gotten messages from movie stars and rap artists – we must be on different lists. She also got a call directing her to the wrong polling place, which she reported to the Cuyahoga County Board of Elections and the *The Plain Dealer*. It seems she wasn't the only one to get such a call. Talk about dirty pool, but I suspect other elections throughout our country's history have been besmirched by similar or even more damaging events – which doesn't make it okay. While I think that my life is strongly shaped by ideals and principles, the real world is a lot messier. Work experience and family relations have shown how easy it is to miscommunicate and misunderstand each other. Coming together and keeping the peace requires navigating a river full of rapids and submerged rocks.

Meanwhile, the Grand River flows on, its supply of water seemingly inexhaustible. Isn't that amazing? The water keeps coming and coming and coming. I understand the science – precipitation, evaporation, aquifers, run-off, etc., but to stand and watch the unceasing flow of a river is one of the world's wonders for me. At least there are some preservation measures in place that has kept our county from turning into a desert like parts of China, where overpopulation, pollution, land use mismanagement, and government corruption have converted farmland into a creeping pile of sand. I've been reading the *National Geographic* again. I'm grateful for every entity that monitors the quality of our rivers and puts protections in place that will last beyond the current generation.

Just as the river valley seems to be preparing itself for the coming cold, we have prepared for winter at home. Our Halloween party on Saturday night was a success with windy but warm weather, a full moon, delicious ham and bean soup, and a roaring fire built inside a trunk section from our hollow old maple that used to stand along the road. Our neighbor cut it down for us in exchange for fireplace wood. I asked him to make his cut six feet off the ground and leave the lower trunk still standing. I thought I would have a carving done by a chainsaw artist like the eagle one neighbor commissioned as a birthday present for his wife. But when I learned the cost, I demurred. Maybe I could do something myself – something abstract that I could claim was art – but the tree was hollow. We had all the hollow pieces cut into two foot sections which made perfect cauldrons for fires as they keep the wind from scattering sparks and flames. Eventually the trunk burns, but the fire was lovely while it lasted on Saturday. Maybe I will plant something in the one foot stump remaining by the roadside.

The lawn furniture has been put away, the screen doors and window screens are stored, and the windows washed. The lawn mower has exchanged positions with the snowblower. The nights are cooler. Clear skies showcase stars and constellations which are reflected in the beautiful and eternal waters of the Grand River.

25 THE SQUEAKY WHEEL

Wednesday, November 9, 10:15 a.m., 38 ° F.

The sun is out. A very blue sky is apparent among the gray-floored cumulus clouds. We have entered the gray days' phase here in Northeast Ohio. According to the National Climatic Data Center, Cleveland has 202 cloudy days each year, as recorded at Hopkins International Airport. Another 97 days are partly cloudy – only 66 are designated sunny. However, there are 39 other U.S.A. cities that have more cloudy days. The top five cloudiest towns are all in Alaska. I feel better already.

After a breakfast of watermelon with tea and toast, I grab my camera and leave without a coat or socks. I figure I'll be out of the car for just a few moments taking my photos at the bridge – I want to catch sunlight on the Grand River. On my way clouds obscure the sun, but I still see white clouds glowing in the north. I continue on in hope that sunshine will still be on the river. A black and white cat scurries across the road.

As I turn right onto Blair Road, I see a sign stating Flagger Ahead. Maybe the road crew is here removing the graffiti. On the second curve down the hill to the bridge, I stop for the uphill flagger. Three trucks and five workers are busy repairing the end of a driveway. No, it's not the work detail to remove the graffiti. I drive on past them to my usual parking place. As I get out of the car and walk to the bridge, I notice the downhill flagger watching me.

The sun is shining, but I forgot that the south bluff prevents the sun's rays from striking the valley floor and river at this hour of the day, especially now that the sun arcs farther south. The only sunlight I capture is in the view downstream where it highlights some barren sycamore trees, throwing their white trunks into sharp contrast with other black trunks, black waters, and black south valley wall. The golden grasses under the sycamore trees copy the river's curve. The clouds are spectacular – large volumes of white fluff hovering over the few still-attached gold and brown leaves on some trees up on the rim. I angle my shot higher than usual. One never knows when one will capture a spectacular image. I have this great photo of pelicans reflected in still water near an island dock, but that's another story.

After turning my car around to go home, I stop just past the workers and their equipment on my way uphill. I ask for the person in charge and am directed to the man in the orange hat with a walkie-talkie in his back pocket. He listens to my complaint about the graffiti under the bridge. Yes, the bridge is the Lake County Engineer's responsibility and thus theirs too since their trucks are clearly marked with that name. He asks me to report it again.

"The squeaky wheel gets the grease. Maybe it will get moved up on the jobs list," he says.

Shouting a thank you (he has ear plugs in situ), I return to my heated car. These guys have on two or three layers of clothing and thick socks inside their work boots. Wimps – try bare toes and jacketless torso sometime.

Home I hurry to make my second round of calls regarding the graffiti problem. The staff at Grand River Partners is in a meeting. The detectives at the sheriff's office are unavailable, probably busy investigating the murder that occurred last night in Painesville. My call to the Lake County Engineer's office (the incumbent was reelected last week) meets some resistance at first. The woman just wants to take my report. I explain that I have already made a report and ask to talk to someone who might know the plans for removing the graffiti. I am then connected to the woman I spoke with two weeks ago; she assures me a work order has been issued and the workers out on Blair Road also just called in about my conversation with them. Hurrah. I share with her information I gleaned from a phone call to the maintenance department at Lakeland Community College. The staff there said it should be reported to the police (I have) and then a pressure washer used to remove the spray paint since it's on concrete. The woman at the Engineer's office doesn't know whether the graffiti paint will be removed or just painted over, but she thinks there is pressure washing equipment lying around. My name and phone number are taken again and a return call is promised.

The sun goes in and out of the clouds. I am reminded of last night's sunset at home – a display of lavender clouds against a red-orange sky. I wonder what the sunsets are like at the Grand River. I would need to be there around 5 p.m. Maybe I should get out our tent and pitch it on the flood plain. Maybe the graffiti sprayer (I have a hard time calling him/her an artist) will return and be caught by me.

26 GRAY AND WHITE

Thursday, November 18, 4:55 p.m., 46° F.

It's a typical northeastern fall day at dusk. Clouds have obscured the sky all day. There's just a hint of blue sky now in the west as I am driving home. Fog hangs on top of the escarpment along River Road then glides into the valleys. I hope there's enough light left today to get my photos at the Blair Road Bridge. I hope the steadily shortening daylight and my work schedule don't interfere with this project.

I love the word escarpment. Derived from French, it is defined as a steep slope or cliff formed by erosion, or less often by faulting. I thought it meant the bank left after a lake receded. I also like the word because it is close to escape, which is what I do in my mind as I envision the prior landscape along River Road when Lake Erie used to lap along its berm. Imagine all the land north being under water – Klyn Nurseries with its specimen trees, the homes, the retail stores along South Ridge, Middle Ridge, and North Ridge Roads (all of which were prior lake edges too), the 'starter castles' being built along Lake Erie's edge, the parks. None would exist if the waters had not receded after the last ice age.

As I approach the Grand River down the north hill and go past the still startling-white trunks of my favorite sycamore tree in the weakening daylight, I search for the south base of the bridge. Is the graffiti gone yet? On Monday when I was going into work, a truck was parked on the south side of the bridge. There was an air compressor in its bed. I almost stopped to thank the workers since I assumed removing graffiti had reached the top of the job stack at the Lake County Engineer's office. But I had only enough minutes left to arrive at work on time. Since I am the supervisor, it's hard to insist other employees show up on time if I don't.

Yes, the graffiti is gone. However it was just painted over – white paint obvious against the gray concrete. At least the painting was done well – the line at the top of the painted section is straight. I was hoping for restoration to the original weathered concrete. Now there will always be a reminder of what changed the scenery under the bridge – at least for me. I'll send a thank-you note tomorrow anyway with a promise to keep an eye on things at the bridge.

Very few leaves remain on the trees along the river. Bare branches reach for the cloudy sky, looking nude and unprotected. The water level seems even lower, exposing more gravel bars. The bank grasses are mostly brown with a hint of green or gold next to the old stones holding up the north end of the bridge. Far away on the north rim, fat, dark evergreen trees appear among the deciduous stick silhouettes. Everything else is gray – gray tree trunks, gray water, gray sky, and gray concrete on the bridge bottom, pillars, and embankments. I drive a gray car. At least I don't have on gray clothes, and the eastern hemlock that I use to frame my westward photo is still a lovely true green even in the fading light of this late fall day.

Below in the river, light rain is speckling the water with silver dots. The air is still and I listen to the gentle pelting of the raindrops – to the ever-so-slightly different tones created by raindrops falling on water, asphalt, cloth or pine needles. The languid river carries music on its back around the bend and on to Lake Erie, where the song is changed by more volume and depth. I wish I had time now to canoe downstream and out onto the lake to hear today's tunes.

I put my bird feeders up last weekend. Anthropomorphically I assumed that the birds who seemed to be dive-bombing the house were trying to tell me it was time to put the feeders on our new wire cable between two maple trees. During my zealous pruning this past spring, I removed the last low branches on the old serviceberry at the edge of the woods where I used to hang all the feeders. My husband wants to try a new arrangement anyway in hopes of giving the squirrels a challenge this winter and I wanted the feeders closer to the gravel pathway so I don't have to wade through snow-covered understory that camouflages slippery branches and mud holes.

After I put up the feeders, I hung around the dining room windows to mark which bird first found this season's offerings. It was a black-capped chickadee, followed closely by a tufted titmouse and then seemingly all the birds in LeRoy Township. I love the flurry of flight and flapping wings of fire engine red, swimming pool blue, and sunflower yellow mixed among the duller gray, black and brown birds.

The Grand River valley at the Blair Road Bridge is a mosaic of brown, gray, and black with some specks of green. And now white, if you are on the north bank and gaze at the south cement embankment under the bridge. This change is still disturbing to me. A white concrete wall doesn't sound like much, but everything counts in human time. I want the river to be free of human harm – to be a diamond ribbon forever freely flowing and admired.

27 FISH AND STUFFING

Wednesday, November 24, 8:06 a.m., 40° F.

Today is the best time this week to stop at the Grand River. Tomorrow is Thanksgiving and we are going to my parents' farm near Lexington, Ohio. Friday we will be back home and preparing for a Saturday Thanksgiving dinner for my husband's relatives.

It's a wonderful fall morning – gray and gloomy with a misty rain. My car lights are needed – not to see, but to let other drivers see me since my silver Honda blends so well with today's gray. The river drifts between its tawny banks; rain that is barely heard creating white dots on its surface. I welcome wetness on my face, but my camera cannot be protected and my photos may be compromised. I breathe deeply the water-laden air and view the valley scene, once again alone at the river.

Wait, I am not alone. There are two men in muted green jackets, hats, and hip-high waders fishing 500 feet upstream. I can hear them talking, their voices like jewel tones in the rain. I wonder if they notice me at the bridge when my camera flashes in the low light. What time did they get up this morning to be here on the river? Are they catching any fish?

The Grand River Partners claim that 74 species of fish inhabit the Grand River. Lake Metroparks state the following game fish can be found all along the Grand River: bluegill, small-mouth bass and steelhead trout (fall to spring only). Just go to these locations: Harpersfield Dam, Hogsback Ridge Park, Riverview Park, Hidden Valley Park, Indian Point Park, Mason's Landing, Painesville City Park and Old Dam or Fairport Harbor's short pier. My Blair Road Bridge site is between Hidden Valley Park and Indian Point Park, so any fish caught here will not swim miles of secluded, bending river water upstream. What are the other 71 fish species?

Several rivers in the United States are named the same as this one I visit weekly. You will find a Grand River in Michigan and Wisconsin. Iowa and Missouri share a Grand River as do North and South Dakota. There's also a Grand River in Ontario, Canada. Anyone fishing on these rivers today? Anyone out looking at their Grand River at this moment?

On my way home from work around 4 p.m., I look for the fishermen, but they are gone – probably home for their own Thanksgiving traditions. And the caught fish – are they part of the Thanksgiving meal or frozen for later?

I wish I were preparing the Thanksgiving meal at my house, but it's become too much for my parents to travel four hours in one day.

They decline to stay over, preferring to sleep in their own bed. And I don't want them traveling on an Ohio Highway Patrol death-watch day. But I miss the last decade's pattern when my parents and sister came to my home.

My father is a meat and potatoes man with definite likes and dislikes, especially with holiday meals. When he was dining with me on Thanksgivings, I would prepare the usual dishes – turkey, mashed white potatoes with gravy, candied sweet potatoes, green beans, and a relish tray of cut raw vegetables, cheese and pickles. My mother would bring the cranberry salad and pumpkin pie. And I would mess with the stuffing. Each year I would add an additional ingredient to the traditional bread cubes, butter, onion, celery, and poultry seasoning. Dad caught on right away.

"This tastes different," he said the first time. "What did you put in the stuffing this time?" became the annual question thereafter. I would insist he taste it first and try to guess the mystery ingredient before I confessed. Over the decade I tired apples, water chestnuts, mushrooms, sausage and walnuts. All were disliked by my father still trying to keep things from changing in his eighties. But he ate the stuffing anyway – even second helpings. It's a good thing he's not going to be here this Saturday. I am adding mushrooms, apples, cilantro, parsley, and asparagus to the stuffing.

The Grand River has its stages – I wouldn't call them traditions. Sometimes it's high and rushing, sometimes it's low and rippling, sometimes its surface is dimpled by rain like today, sometimes the sunlit waters are so bright it is hard to view its beauty and once a week some woman stops and takes photos at the Blair Road Bridge.

28 WALKING THE BRIDGE

Wednesday, December 1, 11:45 a.m., 35° F.

It's a blustery day – or, as *Webster's New World Dictionary* states, one flowing fitfully with violence and noise. The wind and rain woke me several times during the night. This morning, Rana Pond is full and overflowing, water snaking through the backyard swale. The sky is gray with cloud clumps racing northwest to southeast. I might as well get my photos of the Grand River now; the sky could stay like this for days.

Off I go in flannel-lined jeans, a sweater, full-length beige London Fog raincoat, and sandals without socks. I won't be gone long. Broken tree branches litter the roadway and all the ditches are full of water. One neighbor is out cleaning leaves from the drain under his driveway. My Honda is being shoved askew by the wind. At the bridge over Interstate 90, I see what a 'hard day's night' today is for semi-truck drivers.

The river water is high, covering half of my log marker on the eastern bank. The rustling, rippled, rushing water carries tree limbs and leaf litter under the bridge. Diminutive whitecaps lighten the tea with milk-colored water. It feels like the bridge and I are moving too when I gaze at the turbulence below. The dark green hemlock trees are lovely against all the brown, gray, and black here.

I realize I have never walked across the bridge. I have stood partway on it, walked beneath its bed when gravel was exposed along the concrete supports, canoed under it, photographed it, but never just walked across and back. It looks to be about one hundred feet across. So I do – in my open toe-and-heel sandals. The gusty wind's noise as it hits the trees and my coat drowns out any sounds from the river but not the bells marking the quarter hour. It's worth cold feet to hear chimes on a threatening fall day while walking on an asphalt-covered steel bridge above a rushing river.

Daniel Alward, for awhile, had an excellent website on the Grand River's bridges, including pictures of some that no longer exist. There was nothing on the Blair Road Bridge and the website is now gone. Lake County's Bridge Engineer, Kirk Dimmick, tells me that the twenty-four foot wide Blair Road Bridge, constructed in 1999, consists of two seventy-four foot steel spans. When the south foundation collapsed in the 1970s, cement, gravel, and netting were brought in to stabilize the area. The north cut-stone embankment is maintained as such because our county crews still have stone-setting skills. When needed, more stones are acquired from other harvested replacement projects or stone salvage companies. He agrees that the large rectangular stones are aesthetically preferable. (A cut stone foundation was used on a bridge replacement over Mill Creek after the July 2006 flood. See Chapter 59.)

A pickup truck and one car pass by while I am on the bridge. I feel like Jane Eyre with my coattails flapping in the wind, my collar pulled up to frame my face with its blue eyeglasses (Jane didn't wear glasses) and short-cropped hair (Jane's hair was definitely long). Anyway, I'm a mystery woman leaning out over the low railing, peering at the water. Who is she? What's she doing here in her sandals in the middle of a December Wednesday on such an awful day, staring at the water? Is she going to jump? The vehicles go on by.

Back in the car, I turn the heater on full blast before starting up the hill. I have one exposure left on this roll of film. So I will use it on another project I am considering – photos of faces that occur naturally in inanimate objects. Last night I noticed the underside of the lid on the cat food can has a 'face'. Today on my way home, I stop at a decaying tree trunk severed twenty feet above the ground; I can see a face in its bark. I have the Grand River to thank for increasing my observational skills – looking for details in the larger picture. That is what I wanted to happen when I started this project.

Back at my house, the clouds part and sunlight floods my dining room table where I am writing. I'm not going back to the Grand River for a sunny shot; I'll just imagine how grand it looks in the strong light and equally strong wind.

29 A LUCKY DAY

Tuesday, December 7, 1:30 p.m., 57° F.

This day starts in a mundane way but ends magically. First I go to Thompson to mail our 87 holiday cards and one package. I forgot the post office closes for the noon hour, so I eat a cheeseburger and fries at Stocker's Restaurant while waiting. Only two other customers are in the restaurant – those women decide to have chocolate cake with ice cream and so do I.

It rained all morning. Now it's windy and balmy on a day that averages 27-36 degrees F. After mailing my items when the post office reopens, I decide the fastest and least muddy way to the river is by way of Clay Street to Ford and Blair roads. Clay Street was paved this year, but it still looks slick. My car already hydro-planed rounding the square in Thompson. Even though I prefer the slowness that a gravel road requires, enjoy how it often becomes potholed and rutted as the season progresses and like the sound of tires on gravel, pavement is just fine today.

The sky is starting to clear in the south. I see blue and yellow around the northern gray clouds. Just as I park my car at the Blair Road Bridge, sunlight strikes the river and its valley. I rush to the west edge of the bridge to get my photo, and then back to the east to position my camera on the concrete wall. When I lift my camera up to position the final shot north, I notice a rainbow – faint multicolored bands above the bluff's trees. I take another photo and watch as the rainbow fades and white clouds push gray ones eastward. The water ripples and gurgles past as the bell tower chimes an eight-note melody.

I have yet to photograph the bell tower. It's about a thousand feet away and partially hidden by trees at the rim of the southwest bluff. My camera has a zoom lens, but I can't get a clear view from the bridge. I drive across the bridge to the place where the fishermen park. I see more of the bell tower from here but still not enough. At the top of the road's climb, I am directly across from the tower and at the same elevation. I park two feet off the pavement, open my car door and jump out to get a photo while hoping that no other car comes along. But the light is not right. The sun is too close to the tower. I'll have to try again another day. I have not gotten any response to my request to visit Walden II. I'll call the Ohio Nature Conservancy office again today.

To turn the car around now I have to drive farther north. I pick the driveway of a property at the top of the hill where a small fenced-in pasture corrals brown goats. I've been wanting to meet these goats. They pay no attention to me whatsoever, even though I try all kinds of calls, clucks and whistles. The balmy day and green grass win out over a crouching, noisy woman with a flashing light. I know better than to try and touch the goats by reaching through the wood board fence with its electric wires. But their deep rich brown fur with black edging on the ears, spine and feet is so enticing and almost irresistible. Sunlight on the Grand River, a rainbow above the valley, chimes, and goats – how lucky can one person get.

30 THE SNOWBELT

Wednesday, December 15, 8:12 a.m., 12° F.

It's the first big snowfall – twenty inches yesterday. Once in November snow covered the ground but it melted the next day. I didn't go to the Grand River yesterday since I didn't want to creep down the south hill at one mile per hour or end up in the ditch. I could have hiked it from the top of the hill, but I don't trust my left knee. My knee replacement surgery is scheduled for January 21. Eventually I'll be hiking again, I hope.

So on my way to work, I stop for my photos. The salted roads are free of snow. It's cloudy, but the snow-shrouded banks and trees supply light. If there was sunshine today, I would need sunglasses. The amount of snow seems less here than at my home. The water is high – my fallen log seat on the northeast bank has only its root ball tips and vertical branches visible.

At this fourteen foot high Blair Road Bridge, the Grand River flows in the first valley after the last Lake Erie escarpment. The riverbed elevation is 644 feet above sea level and the bluffs average 788-800 feet above sea level. My house at 1010 feet elevation is on the next plain and only three miles from the local high point of 1270 feet at Thompson. All of these sites are higher than the 574 elevation of Lake Erie's shoreline, creating the perfect topography for a snowbelt of lake-effect snow.

A cold air mass coming over warmer Lake Erie increases evaporation. Once moistened, the air mass becomes unstable and moves upward resulting in clouds and precipitation, especially when it runs into my county's higher terrain. If it's cold enough, we get snow. Since there are no mountains between Lake Erie and Lake Huron, any moisture gained by north or northwest winds crossing Lake Huron passes over southwest Ontario to join Lake Erie's collection before dumping on northeast Ohio hills. If it's cold enough, we get even more snow. Isn't that just so cool?

The snowbelt starts in the eastern suburbs of Cleveland and extends all along extreme northeastern Ohio into northwestern Pennsylvania and western New York. And I live right in the middle of all of that just about 10 miles north of Chardon, which prides itself on being the snowiest Ohio town. The snowfall there is about 50 percent more than what is recorded at Hopkins International Airport in Cleveland. Records kept from 1952 to present shows that Chardon averaged 107 inches of snow per year while Cleveland averaged fifty-four inches. The snowfall at my house is close to that of Chardon's and sometimes even surpasses it since I am nearer the high point of Thompson and only a few miles from the Madison escarpment at the edge of the Grand River Valley. But the closest records are those on chardon.cc/snowfall.html.

The risk for heavy snow in November and December is higher in the snowbelt than elsewhere in Ohio because Lake Erie takes a while to cool. During December, Lake Erie starts to freeze first at its shallow western end. By late February, an average of 90-100% of the lake is frozen solid. One would think the lake-effect snow would end then, but snowfall averages are still greater because of occasional openings in the ice and higher elevations inland. Even if Lake Erie did not exist, the higher elevation creates more snow because this region can also experience Atlantic coastal storms, which roam as far inland as eastern Ohio. But without Lake Erie, Ohio's snowbelt would average fifty-one inches of snow per year, similar to Cleveland. Hurray for Lake Erie and the ridges and the valleys inland. It gives us more snow overall and more continuously on the ground.

About four inches of snow cover is needed to cross-country ski or use a noisy snowmobile. It's also enough to insulate the soil. About 52 winter days have such conditions. Unfortunately, pollutants also accumulate in snow packs, particularly increased sulfate concentrations resulting in acidic meltwater. Let it snow, but let's stop our polluting.

I hope there's enough light today to get my photos. My first one is hampered by two feet of plowed snow in front of the cement waist-high wall where I like to place my camera. I stand at the pavement's edge instead. Ah, the challenges changing weather brings, and winter doesn't officially arrive for six more days.

The landscape is black and white. Whatever green grasses may be left on the ground are covered by snow. The river writhes like a large black snake between its white banks. The barren trees stand out distinctly against the white backdrop as they lift their dark branches into the gray sky. Even the visible shale wall to the east is spattered with a light dusting of snow that in the faint light of early morning becomes a gray wall. Twelve degrees Fahrenheit feels very cold; fortunately the wind is light. Ruffles on the water are from the river's flow – not the breezes. This would be a trying time to sit an hour by the river.

Even with the sunshine, it's a relief to get back into my running, warmed car for the rest of my ride to work. There are no tracks in the barnyard at the top of the north hill; the goats must be inside. I suspect they won't be outside again until the snow melts and the ground thaws. Let it snow, let it snow. I welcome the light and beauty it brings to the more frequent sunless days ahead.

On my way home from work around 4:45 p.m., the sun is still shining but not on the bell tower. While it's more visible through the bare trees, sunlight would help highlight its perch on the south rim. At the bridge I stop to take another set of photos. Sunshine on the northern and eastern trees highlights their brown trunks and branches against the snow-covered ground and bluffs. The sky has a blue cast, and so does the river's east water but downstream where the high south bluff keeps everything below it in shadow, a black snake still leads west.

As I write on the weekend, another snowstorm has blown in from the north. Four inches of snow have obliterated the driveway – a foot more is predicted. The temperature hovers around ten degrees F. Rana Pond has been frozen for a week. I need knee-high boots when restocking the bird feeders or retrieving the newspaper.

I wish I had a job that didn't require me to drive in the winter. I long for a winter where I choose to stay home except for obtaining provisions. If I were a farmer, I could be inside except for feeding livestock. Either I am channeling some ancestors or I was born in the wrong century to suit my temperament. However, I wouldn't want to give up this era's life expectancy or health care advantages. You can't have it all, but maybe the Grand River can if it's preserved and protected.

Coming home from a holiday party on Friday around 10 p.m., my car passes an SUV stopped just north of the Blair Road Bridge. Two people are lashing two canoes on the roof of the vehicle. Who in the world was canoeing down the Grand River at this time of night in this weather? Oh, wow, what an experience that would be. I hope they are going home to mugs of hot chocolate. The Grand River will continue its cooling process as winter arrives. When will I see the first ice on this storied water?

31 RIVER ICE AND ACCESS

Monday, December 20, 10:20 a.m., 12° F.

There's ice in the Grand River – I'll call it pebble ice. Clumps of ice the size of small, flat stones and slightly beige/yellow from the water's organic matter flow in the main channel of the swift current hurrying on to Painesville. The sides of the river, especially on the curves where the water is calmer, are also ice-covered. On the north shore only one-half of the river water is visible. I didn't expect to see anything of significance today, but temperatures have been below freezing for about five days. Is the ice forming first along the river banks in a continuous shelf at whose edges the current nibbles to make my pebble ice, or is the ice forming everywhere on the water at the same time?

According to *Wikipedia*, ice is a mineral, a solid that is eight percent less dense than liquid water. That's a good thing because then ice floats. When subjected to higher pressures and varying temperatures, everyday ice and snow, called hexagonal ice (Ih), can form in roughly a dozen different phases from ice Ic (cubic crystalline) all the way to ice XII – a tetragonal, metastable, dense crystalline phase – that's a mouthful.

I'm partial to more common descriptive terms like black ice, frazil ice, sea ice, or glacier ice. How about polynya (a body of water surrounded by sea ice) or Europa (an ice-covered moon)? Rime is a type of ice formed by fog freezing on cold objects. Icicles are formed as water drips, then refreezes – duh. Pancake ice (my pebble ice?) is generally created in less calm conditions. And if one wants to drive vehicles on lake or river ice, wait until it is at least thirty centimeters (one foot) thick.

The scene at the Grand River today is a panorama of black and white, including the overcast sky – so much so that the beige/yellow cast of the flowing ice seems bright. I'm grateful for my down jacket with its fur-trimmed hood as I move across the road to take my west photo. The eastern hemlock on my left adds a touch of color, but its green almost looks black today.

The goats at the top of the north hill are still inside their barn. I go on to work and wonder off and on about the ice. Why do I find it so much more calming and satisfying to consider nature than people? Is it because of its seeming permanence, or is it the lack of speech? I was going to say silence, but there is little silent about nature, although it may seem so at times.

People are complaining about the cold and snow as if this doesn't happen every year. I'm hoping for a white Christmas with below freezing temperatures. Colby put up new pot lights on the split-rail fence edging Rana Pond. Those along with blue floodlights on the back deck turn a snow-covered yard and frozen pond into a winter wonderland visible outside our large dining room windows.

I've mentioned my weekly visits to the Grand River to several friends. They all express interest, but not enthusiasm. Maybe just one of them will become more observant of a favorite nature view because of my project. It seems so many people go through life without any connection to nature except that which is forced upon them. But New York City just experienced the wrath of nature lovers.

A red-tailed hawk, Pale Male, and his current mate, Lola, have been nesting for many years on top of a chic, high-rise, Fifth Avenue apartment building across from Central Park. Mary Tyler Moore is one of the apartment's notable residents. The hawks' fan club watches them through binoculars from the park's perimeter. Although protected by the Migratory Bird Act, the building's owner asked and got permission from the U.S. Fish and Wildlife Service to remove the nest. It was "unsightly," "unused," and the birds dropped "carcasses" on the sidewalk. When the nest was destroyed, citizens nationwide (Colby and I joined the e-mail blitz) protested the action to the Fish and Wildlife Service. They agreed to "restore" the nest along with an apron to catch falling debris. Now let's hope that Pale Male and Lola won't mind the new steel base.

It is great that cities and counties now seem to value their wild spots more and plan for walkways, trails, parks, and access to lakes. Cleveland has the magnificent Emerald Necklace of parks that flows through the city and around Cuyahoga County in almost a continuous semicircle. Way back in 1916, William Stinchcomb, a young, self-taught engineer, proposed the need for open space in growing Cleveland. Inspired by his vision, the Cleveland Metropolitan Park District, born in 1917, took on the task of establishing a series of parks and parkways at the perimeter of the city that would be linked by its primary boulevards. Stinchcomb wanted the parklands, which were to follow the stream and river beds or ravines and gullies, to be a short drive for all of the county's people.

The Park District, with public support and private donations of river valley lands, followed the plan unit by unit, resulting in the almost completed Necklace of today with its 19,000 acres and twelve reservations. Four neighboring counties are now also included. The western end of the necklace fails to reach Lake Erie, and there is a gap in parkland on the eastern leg, but all the other reservations are contiguous. Recently the old Dike 14 landfill on the east became the Lakefront Nature Preserve. Movement has commenced again to complete the Necklace as originally proposed.

But public access to Lake Erie in downtown Cleveland is still sparse and fragmented. Many plans have been proposed over the years by various politicians and interested parties, but rarely does anything happen. Within the last year there were five new proposals outlined in *The Plain Dealer*. I loved the one that would turn the breakwall into a sliver of greenery with a walking trail but that idea was not adopted. I'm only hoping that something will happen. Time will tell – we need another William Stinchcomb.

In Lake County where I live and visit the Grand River at the edge of LeRoy Township, there are seven parks on the shores of Lake Erie, and 23 other parks, facilities, and properties inland – all part of the Lake Metroparks. Formed in 1958 by some visionary citizens of the smallest county in Ohio, the park district now encompasses 7,289 acres, 83 percent owned outright. The Grand River flows by only one of the Lake Erie shoreline parks, the one at its mouth called the Fairport Harbor Lakefront Park Beach.

The river has its own set of parks. Geauga County has Chickagami Preserve within the headwaters of the Grand River watershed. Trumbull County's MetroParks focuses on the Mahoning River, but there is land preserved along the Grand River – 7,453 acres within the Grand River Wildlife Area owned and operated by the Ohio Department of Natural Resources. Established in 1956, the area contains 12 ponds, many beaver impoundments, and over 30 man-made marshes covering 300 acres. Five tributary streams flow into the river in this region which is about 46 percent second growth hardwoods, 49 percent open land with brush and rotated crops to benefit wildlife, and five percent wetlands and river. The Ohio Department of Natural Resources cautions even experienced outdoorsmen that one can get lost here.

It is here that the river otter was reintroduced in 1986-1988. The otter population has increased so dramatically since then that its endangered species status was removed, and in 2005 Ohio had its first river otter trapping season. The primary purpose of the wildlife area was to provide public hunting and fishing, but now hiking and bird watching are just as popular. The marshes encourage waterfowl to land and nest during the fall migration and lots of other bird species take advantage of the semi-wilderness.

In Ashtabula County only the Harpersfield Covered Bridge Metropark and the Fobes Road Township Park border the river, but pockets of preserved land like the Grand River Terraces, Morgan Swamp (Nature Conservancy) and Ashcroft Woods (Western Reserve Land Conservancy) exist along its banks. Lake County has six parks: Hogback Ridge, Riverview Park, Hidden Valley Park, Indian Point Park, Mason's Landing, and the Fairport Harbor Lakefront Park previously mentioned.

(Since this date Lake Metroparks has acquired and named two more

82

parcels – no public access: Conley Paradise Road Metropark, and my beloved location, Blair Road Metropark. I am so happy that both flood zones along the road north of the Blair Road Bridge are preserved. I wonder what plans, if any, Lake Metroparks has for these 61.93 acres. However, the southeastern flood zone formed by the river's oxbow upstream is owned by Blair Road Investments, Inc. I cannot find any information about this entity, but hope it was set up for preservation and not development although its name suggests the later. It would require a lot of manipulation to make that land suitable for homes which would potentially harm the river and ruin the view. I hope there are enough county, state, and EPA regulations to stop such a move.)

The river feels largely connected and valued although you cannot walk along its whole length. As I gaze at its cold waters and gifts of ice, I am glad for every inch that is public or protected. May there be more and more walking trails, I think, but I'm not sure that's best for the river even though I would love to walk along it from beginning to end. Ninety-eight and a half miles? How long would it take to make that journey? In my mind's eye, I see the shape of the Grand River and a lone figure with a backpack moving along its bank.

32 CLIMBING THE HILLS

Monday, December 27, 10:30 a.m., 6° F.

Our Christmas holidays have been white and cold just like I wanted. Over thirty inches of snow covers the picnic table on my upper deck – a new record for us. There's a narrow trail from the door to the outside stairs which Emmett deigns to navigate occasionally for a little outside time. Mostly he flees back to the house and his litter box when presented with the cold air blast from an opened door. Who can blame him?

I walk another trail in my knee-high boots from the downstairs back door to the bird feeders. Colby has done most of the snowblowing; our driveway is now bordered by four-foot high snow banks. I absolutely love it. My daughter and friend took a walk with me to the valley edge of the Hell Hollow Wilderness Area about ¾ of a mile by road. They went downhill on the old eroded roadbed to Paine Creek; I turned around. Until my left knee is replaced, any prolonged hiking, particularly on rough, hilly terrain, leads to twenty-four hours or more of pain.

At the Grand River this morning, I see more ice that looks like pancakes or lily pads. The water is high – up to my fallen trunk perch on the north bank and covering all but the root ball of my other benchmark trunk across the water. Snow covers everything including the sheets of ice creeping out from the little calm coves. Piled snow forces me to stand so far back from the cement abutment that my shot north along the bridge does not include the open water. In the east and west views, the black river glides between banks punctuated by black trees with white branches. There's no wind, so six degrees F. doesn't feel frigid, but my ungloved hands gripping the camera know it's cold. The sun is shining in between large cumuli so that blue tops the sights here and there. It's almost silent. I wish I could stay longer, but I'm on my way to work as usual, and the cold would chase me away soon anyway.

Last night Colby and I stopped by his cousin's home in Painesville to see her new grandson. We ooh'ed and ah'ed along with the 30 other guests, then left for home along River Road to Blair Road. It had been snowing all evening, covering the roads with a slick inch of fresh snow on top of what was already there. When we got to the bottom of the north hill at the Grand River, there was a car stopped on our right and another car approaching from the bridge. After the oncoming car passed, we stopped too. I rolled down my window and asked the occupants of the stopped car if they needed any help.

The car had four passengers, all less than thirty years of age. The driver explained that both he and the other car that just passed us couldn't get up the south hill. I replied, "So it's our turn," and should have added "Leave it to the old folks." I wish I had as Colby spun and slide triumphantly to the top of the hill. Our climb was visible to the stalled car below through the bare trees. I checked the rearview mirror several times for car lights, but didn't see any. A warm superior glow existed inside our car. I wonder when and which hill they finally conquered to get out of the valley. I hope they considered it an adventure like I do.

Thinking of the Grand River now, I visualize snow-covered banks and trees beside icy waters. Warmer weather is predicted for the end of this week – the newspaper forecasts temperatures in the 50s. And where does all that melting snow go? Across our lawns and fields into road ditches and gullies that join the creeks ending at the Grand River. There should be some great river-viewing this weekend and possibly flooding.

33 CLOSINGS AND CROSSINGS

Monday, January 3, 2005, 10:48 a.m., 36° F.

At breakfast Colby says, "The river should be high today." It has been raining for twelve hours. After four days of warm weather – anything above freezing counts – most of our thirty inches of snow has melted except for where it was piled by snowblowers or snowplows. That snow is dingy like my Rana Pond's floating gray ice lid.

I grab a wide-brimmed straw hat to keep the rain off my camera and drive to my usual parking spot at the Blair Road Bridge. Colby was right. The river extends onto its flood zones, covering my log marker on the southeast bank and surrounding my log seat across the river. It extends onto the lawn in front of the A-frame house. Downstream freshets run down the south bluff in several places, their splashing audible above the howling, rushing brown water, the volume so huge one would think a dam had burst upstream. However, this spill doesn't stop – a never ending stupendous flow. The river is the color of tea with milk, or a latte with a hint of foam.

I snap my usual photos and then proceed to get photos of a freshet, the almost submerged log seat, and the encroaching water near the homes. What is that red and yellow pole over by the A-frame building? It's over twenty feet high with a round ball on top. Is it a flag pole or a flood marker?

If I lived here, I would have a flood marker like the county road department does at the Vrooman Road Bridge, a slender white board with painted black numbers one to eight spaced a foot apart. You see it heading north just after crossing the Grand River on the skeletal metal bridge – a daily reminder that this is a flood zone which fills predictably after heavy rains or rapid snow melts. When Vrooman Road becomes submerged, barricades are pulled onto the roads at the top of the valley walls and people adjust their travel routes. The Road Closed due to Flooding signs are never carted away but just dragged off the pavement where they await the next flooding.

I know the county government plans to replace the Vrooman Road valley bottom bridge in the near future with a high one extending from one bluff to the other for our convenience. It will be an 1800-foot long, high-level valley bridge with two lanes plus shoulders. EPA studies are still pending because the selected site involves park land, wetlands, American Indian burial grounds and a Scenic river section. Some residents are angry about the proposed reshaping of their rural road and potential truck traffic; unfortunately, there is already an Interstate 90 intersection about five miles south. The proposed bridge will be straight across the valley, which will indeed improve the topside intersection geometry – no more steep north hill with a traffic light at the top where you hope your brakes will hold until you can gun your car through on the green light. And gone too will be the romantic twists and turns of the south road that starts to rise out of the valley just after Seeley Road branches off east into Indian Point Park.

But I would like to keep the romance, the adventure, the sense of struggle. The muddy rampaging river so aptly named the Grand, the detour while craning our necks to see if anyone got stuck – it's these things that heighten the day and make for a story if you are late to work. It's detouring that breaks the routine. Give me a good flood, give me inconvenience, give me unpredictable weather, and give me a Vrooman Road bridge in the flood zone. I like crossing that bridge, looking at low water in the summer and remembering the spring gift just past – the awesome water that surged to the surrounding bluffs only to pull back. And please leave that eight-foot high-water marker to remind us each normal day of the possibility of floods. Fortunately there are no homes at the Vrooman Road Bridge, only Mason's Landing Metropark, which suffers little from the periodic cleansings.

I have never known the Blair Road Bridge to be closed. There seems to be ample space for any overflow water. The Blair Road river crossing used to be further east, shorter and steeper, perhaps at the end of Abbey Road which no longer crosses the river but still has a visible old roadbed. The private property there recently came up for sale and Colby and I took advantage of the sale to walk down to the river by the old roadbed just to see what was there. It wasn't that steep. So maybe some other old unused roadbed on another property is the prior river crossing. Wherever it was, the *History of Leroy* relates the story of Charlotte Paine who risked crossing the Blair Road Bridge in a horse and buggy after heavy rains. Although advised not to cross by men who were watching the rising river, she did and turned to see the bridge tumble into the river as she was going up the north hill which was tiered in three levels so that horses could rest on their way up. I wonder if she needed a rest too.

Historically and unbelievably, the Grand River was once used for hauling cargo. Beginning in March 1800, the *Gregory*, a five by 35-foot flat-bottomed boat, shipped out of Harpersfield and soon other boats followed. I cannot imagine any boat of that size plying the river today on the frequent low water.

The Grand River roars today, its sound mesmerizing. I'm in the middle of the bridge when I notice Slender Woman at the rear of my parked car. Oh, no, the Tudor house resident is trying to get out of her driveway. "I'm coming," I yell, but the water's noise probably drowns my words. She returns to her car and starts to back-up just as I leap into mine. I wave hurriedly, but she is focused on her driving. I did leave enough room for her to exit, but a truck is coming down the south hill. I bolt onto the road after the truck before her Jeep reaches me.

I've never seen so much traffic. Three vehicles passed me on the bridge while I was taking photos in my straw hat in the rain. Now three more cars pass before I can turn around at the pull-off on the north hill. The Slender Woman must have gone south because her car does not go pass. Maybe one day I will get a chance to speak to her. Roar on, Grand River; I'll be back.

34 SLENDER MAN AND SLENDER WOMAN

March 18, 2007

I meet with Slender Man and Slender Woman who live in the Tudor House on the south bank of the Grand River next to the Blair Road Bridge. They graciously agreed to an interview after I left a note in their mailbox. It's a Sunday morning when I knock on their front door. Slender Man (Jim) opens the door and welcomes me in while assuring me the small dog and big dog will settle down. We walk in and around the low-ceilinged front room and hallway to an eating area just off the kitchen. Fireplace, dark wood beams, and paned windows – it all looks authentic. Slender Lady (Chris) is waiting at the table.

Seventeen years ago they were considering moving out of Painesville, where both teach at Lake Erie College, but had not found anything yet that pleased them. Jim had been canoeing down the Grand River when a fish jumped into his boat. Around the next bend he saw a For Sale sign in front of this house. Figuring the fish was an omen he finished canoeing back to Painesville, jumped on his bicycle and pedaled back out. When he arrived, the real estate agent happened to be there. And the rest is history.

The house had not been occupied for over two years; the owner and his girlfriend preferred to live above his bar. Although in good condition, the house was filled with military garb and guarded by a large dog. When Chris and Jim moved in (after the garb and dog were gone), they had to persuade fauna (rats, snakes, insects, etc.) to move out.

Their first year turned out to be both magical and scary. When friends came for a new owners' celebratory dinner, a 'kettle' happened, according to one biologist guest. Three to four hundred hawks ascended above the river in a circular thermal tunnel for hundreds of feet before flying over the valley walls. At the same time about 200 motorcycles crossed over the Blair Road Bridge. The hawks paid no mind to the motorcyclists. We speculate that maybe The Louie Run, a local charitable event, was routed over the bridge that year. Neither event has happened again, separately or together.

The scary part happened when the ice broke up that first spring and piled up on the banks, scaling fifteen feet up to the mere ten feet of land that lies between the back of their house and the river's edge. Jim and Chris bought flood insurance but only for one year.

They love living here even though they are last on the electricity and phone lines, and can't get TV cable service. They rarely go away on vacations. I go on a tour of the house with Jim, in and out of small rooms on the first floor, viewing the formal living room with its stone fireplace, a classy dining room with wainscoting, and the old kitchen with its back door out onto a stone patio that has a view of the Blair Road Bridge.

The house was built in 1920 by a "guy from England" who used Case Western Reserve University students to duplicate an English Tudor house. It took 10 years to complete the structure. Jim and Chris have made changes. The kitchen was moved to a new location and modernized, but its dark cabinets and deep-toned brown granite countertops fit the original style. A semi-circular alcove with a copper roof and large windows was added to accommodate a table and chairs. The changes seem to have always belonged to the house.

Next to this area is the converted garage. A large space with multiple paned windows floor to ceiling where the doors used to be, the room holds a baby grand piano, assorted comfortable seating including one long couch, and bookcases. Two large rectangular windows in the north wall overlook the river. Outside each window hangs a bird feeder. Because the house is so close to the river, all you see is the water, the far bank, and the bluff face unless you step to the edge of the windowsill and look down. How wonderful.

"The best view is from the bathroom windows upstairs," Jim says.

So up the stairs we go, both dogs following, to see the river from the bathroom. Originally the ceiling sloped so that even Jim (who is shorter than my five feet, six inches) would bump his head getting out of the tub. So a dormer was added, which allowed two rectangular windows side by side that look down on the Grand River. He is right – this is the best view so far. I'd be tempted to put a chair right there.

"Can you hear the river from inside the house?"

"Yes, if the windows are open."

I see the guest bedroom on the west end, the view of the bridge from the second story deck, the office tucked in under the eaves, the master bedroom with its own stone fireplace (whose bed the dogs claim immediately), and the third bedroom before descending a second set of stairs back to the kitchen.

We talk more. In the summer, the river gets very shallow and one time at dusk, a male canoeist called out to them, "How far to Vrooman Road? I told my wife I would be there by now." Seeing as how he had several hours of canoeing left, Jim drove him there instead. His wife was waiting with the police, having assumed her husband was missing. The next morning a note with twenty dollars was left in Jim and Chris's mailbox.

The river has frozen every year except one since they moved in. The year they saw a snowmobile coming upstream, Jim went cross-country skiing on the ice. Chris wonders aloud if anyone has ever been killed on this stretch of the Grand River. They see lots of fishermen wading below their windows, but they are never a problem.

"They respect the land and water," Jim says.

The highest water (seventeen and a half feet) they have seen flowing through the valley was during the last flood (Chapter 59). Jim knows that the first indentation at the bottom of the middle cement bridge pier is eight feet from the river bottom. Each additional line adds another two feet to the depth.

"The water didn't reach the bottom of the bridge; but it was close. Fifteen of the 26 wood steps off our patio were under water," Jim says.

We go outside to the patio, a lovely expanse of pavers and grass under large trees beyond the east end of the house. A picnic table's metal frame awaits its glass top.

"This is where we spend all our time in the summer," Chris says.

The river view is continuous from the large bend slightly east until the water is hidden by the corner of the house. I am so jealous, until he starts talking about how humid it can get. I hadn't thought of that – airflow trapped between two high bluffs and a wide river. Pluses and minuses to everything.

It is on this patio that I make a discovery. What I thought was an A-frame house on the east flat is actually a barn. The owners live in another building, a ranch house a third of the way up the bluff. The vegetation is so dense and the siding so dark it is hard to see the ranch home, even from here. Only its driveway is visible from the road. The barn is used for storage. And parties?

Jim and Chris are the right people to be living here. I can tell they love the house, land and river as we talk about wildlife sightings. Jim is a birder. An Old Squaw duck is the rarest species he has seen. There are lots of snakes – splotchy northern water ones, and black ones, which "bite consistently and often." They were told there were no leaches in the water, but some children found out otherwise when sitting in one summer's slow-moving water. They rescued a turtle off the road with a shovel. They are in love with the soft shelled ones that sunbathe on the river banks. One's shell measured nine and a half inches in length. They see fox, lots of ducks, great blue herons, bald eagles, and many warblers during the migrations; they hope to see a river otter someday. They have not seen a bear. Dogs show up. They wanted to keep Thorton, the Norwegian elkhound, but he went on his way.

They hear and see car accidents on the curving steep road behind their house – mostly drivers going off the road when it snows. They used to offer help, but now they wait to see if the driver lifts a cell phone to his/her ear. And what they would really like to have is an aerial view of their home. Colby will be flying this summer. Maybe I could surprise Jim and Chris with an aerial photo of their house and the Blair Road Bridge - just as long as the pilot doesn't bank too sharply over the Grand River. (Unfortunately, Colby decided to sell the Cessna before I ever got around to getting a photo for them.)

Taken July 28 at Hour Sit

35 CLOUDY AND GRAND

Monday, January 10, 8 a.m., 41° F.

Yesterday would have been a great day to take my photos. Snow covered everything except any open water; it was a winter wonderland. But I was so glad to have a weekend to read and nap that I resisted the urge to drive to the Grand River. Now it's Monday and the temperature rose enough overnight to liquefy all the snow on the trees. The ground is still white, but the picture-perfect postcard opportunity is gone.

I'm on my way to work. The house in the woods on the right at the top of Blair Road's south hill always bugs me whenever I pass it. It sits about 500 feet off the road with a huge number of windows facing northwest and a large deck contiguous from the house to the detached garage. I think it's a lovely building; I just don't like its new beige color. Previously it was a deep bluish-gray and I had to strain then to see the home through the trees, even in winter; that color was a good choice for the setting.

However, the new owners, besides selecting a beige color, removed all the trees within fifty feet of the house and sold off two or three lots on the east and west sides. So now, everything is visible in the summer, and in the winter the house is startling. I wonder if I would be aggravated if I had never seen how the house looked before with trees close enough to shade it in the summer and lower air-conditioning costs. Of course, more sunlight in the winter lowers heating bills. I guess this is why the expression 'each to his own' exists. I just hope they don't plan to sell off any more of their acreage.

The water at the Grand River has receded from its flood zones. Five feet of brown vegetation is visible at each bank before the snow cover begins – land that was underwater last week. The freshets have ceased, but the river is still full and roaring. No one comes by as I snap my photos. The sky is gray, gray, and gray.

I've lived in Lake County since 1974 and have gotten so used to our cloudy winters that I am surprised when we drive south to visit my parents in Lexington and encounter sunshine either by Cleveland's southern suburbs or after Cuyahoga National Park. Here are some definitions for labeling daytime skies. In order to call it sunny or clear, either there are no clouds at all or they cover less than 1/10 of the visible atmosphere. Scattered indicates that an average of 1/10 to 5/10s of the sky has clouds. It's broken if 5/10s to 9/10s of the sky is covered, and overcast when the clouds cover 9/10 or more of the space overhead.

So maybe partly cloudy is synonymous with scattered, cloudy with broken, and heavily clouded with overcast. And to confound it further, the National Weather Service assigns a number from zero to ten based on the sky cover in tenths. In that rating, zero to three denotes a clear day, from four to seven partly cloudy, and from eight to ten cloudy. Now you too can try to be an expert, but I predict someone will undoubtedly correct you.

I do not have a photo of the entire Blair Road Bridge. I have one exposure left, so I back up and shoot a view of the bridge from the south looking north. The yellow and black warning sign will seem jarring against the serene mint green bridge with its silver railings. I wish the warning sign could be lower, maybe affixed to the beginning of the railing itself, but in a heavy snowstorm it might get covered up by plowed snow. I suppose the bridge won't look like much of anything in the photo. And a picture of a gray sky won't be impressive either, but any day at the Grand River is a good day.

Such a bland name Grand River seems unless one has seen what it is describing or speaks it in French – Le Grand Reverie. Either the French were everywhere or many pioneers thought the words were just right, because in addition to the other rivers with the same name that I mentioned before, there are three Grand River towns in the United States. One Grand River is at the northwest mouth of this river, the second in Louisiana and the third in Iowa. There are 11 townships thus named in Ohio, Louisiana and Iowa plus one in Kansas. If there's a river, there's a name. Whoever settled along its banks often extended the river's name onto land, usually usurping any Indian names.

Obviously I feel the Grand River is grand, so the name works for me. The more I learn about it, the more I observe it and sit still beside it, the grander it becomes. On Tuesday I can't resist stopping at the Blair Road Bridge for another set of photos; the sun is shining.

36 FRANKS'S PLACE

Friday, January 14, 3:00 p.m., 20° F.

I want to see the high water again. Colby and I are ready to leave for our weekend destination but we are early, so I suggest we take a side trip down Blair Road to get my photos. I am driving because he is expecting a work-related conference call at 3:30 p.m. I aim toward my usual parking spot, and he worries aloud that I will be blocking the Tudor house driveway – been there and figured it out. He sees my car fits.

It's a cold and blustery day. New snow fell overnight, but at the river there is only a thin white coating on the bluffs and some of the trees. Sunlight sparkles off the brown swirling, rushing water, which covers my log seat. I can just make out a few squiggly roots from the base poking through the surface. Water surrounds the first trees on the north bank. The two bottom rows of the cut stones under the north end of the bridge are under water. I'm guessing the river is at least six feet deep. It is magnificent. I have never seen the water this high.

The wind whips my coat hood against my neck as I cross the road for the west view. From here I see and hear the water divided by the bridge column crash back together. I would love to stay and watch; I could lift my hood, pull the drawstrings tight, and let the wind try to enter the back of my down-filled jacket. Easy for me to say when I know I have to leave.

We are off to the Louis Penfield House in Willoughby Hills. One of nine Usonian ("for the masses") homes in Ohio designed by Frank Lloyd Wright, it is the only one that permits weekend and overnight stays – just bring your personal belongings and some victuals. Louis Penfield, a painter and acquaintance of Mr. Wright, commissioned the home to accommodate his six foot, eight inch height. This one has high doorways whereas Wright preferred low entryways. Built in 1955, the house was never finished internally once the allotted $25,000 budget was reached. After Penfield's divorce, his ex-wife rented it out for five years. Upon Doris's death in 1983, their son Paul inherited the property and he restored the house as Frank Lloyd Wright intended it, even cutting down trees on the thirty acres to make benches as drawn in the framed blueprint that hangs just inside the front entrance. The house was placed on the National Register of Historic Places in 1997. Louis Penfield, who lived until 2002, was able to view the authentically completed house before it was opened for weekend stays in 2003. Interestingly, Louis had also commissioned plans for a second home that would be farther from the undesired Interstate 90 that invaded the north end of his property. Paul and his wife, Donna, now plan to have that house built when they get the money. Frank Lloyd Wright died two weeks after completing the second house plans.

Colby and I and another couple stayed at the Louis Penfield House one weekend last May and fell in love with it. The house may be small and not equipped for us modern dwellers (half-sized refrigerator, no dishwasher, no TV), but its design, décor, and setting create a Zen-like experience. We wanted to experience it again, this time in winter. It also happens to be Colby's birthday tomorrow.

Halfway there, I realize that I forgot the reservation letter and gate instructions. We better go back for them. Colby's conference call is due in less than 10 minutes. Cell phone service varies in our township, even though two more towers have gone up recently. Staying in the car with me as I backtrack for the letter might interrupt his call. We are near the Quail Hollow Resort, so I leave him and his phone in its lobby by a fireplace. When I return with the papers, he continues his conference call in the car, timely concluding it just as we arrive at the Penfield House. After reading the instructions he swings the red, iron gate wide and drives to the house.

From its second floor hallway I catch a glimpse of the Chagrin River about 1000 feet away beyond the lawn and trees. On its east bluff a black band marks the recent reach of a fuller river. Above that band is snow. Between the river and the house, all depressions are filled with water creating a collection of reflecting pools.

We have the house to ourselves until 8 p.m. We spend the time gazing out the floor-to-ceiling living room windows. Three deer come to eat exposed grass under a white pine thirty feet away. Once in a while I climb the stairs to view again the Chagrin River flowing heartily toward Lake Erie. I feel at home here and hope someone is paying attention to this river as I do the Grand River. Tomorrow morning we will walk the lawn and meadow to the Chagrin River. No trip to the Penfield House is complete without a visit to its neighboring river.

37 HILLS, ICE AND KNEE

Thursday, January 20, 8:15 a.m., 17° F.

I spend a few extra minutes at the Blair Road Bridge today even though I am on my way to work. I'm having my left knee replaced tomorrow and don't know when I'll be back. It's another cloudy, gray day. The temperatures have been below freezing for a few days. Fortunately, no breeze stirs my exposed hair, but my breath is visible and my fingers grow cold quickly on the metal camera.

The scene around me is black and white with only the deep green conifers adding color. Dinner plate-sized ice floats lazily on the black water. Sheets of ice, looking like huge, mittened fingers, have formed on the slower flowing river curves. Their widths vary from mere inches to five or six feet in diameter. If this below-freezing weather continues without a break, the Grand River may completely freeze over. How could I have crossed this river routinely for 17 years without recalling if it ever totally freezes over?

Perhaps it's because in this hilly area in winter all eyes are on the roads. If there is any snow or ice on the pavement I must decide at the intersection of Ford and Blair Roads when coming from the south or at the intersection of River and Blair Roads when coming from the north if I am going to hazard the valley hills to the Grand River. Neither hill is visible from the crossroads. Once committed, one could turn around at the last moment on the south brim, but the north side's options for reversing one's course are already on the steep incline.

Ideally, I should make the decision at the end of my driveway. Turning left commits me to either the Blair Road hill or the shorter but just as steep hill after Paine Creek Falls. Turning right commits me to State Route 86 and the big, curvy hill into Painesville past Helen Hazen Wyman Park. (A new straighter, less steep road now climbs out of that valley – not as beautiful as a winding road but there's a terrific view at its top when coming from the north.) Since there is no flatland way out of LeRoy Township, one just chooses between degrees of difficulty and the likelihood that the county road crew with their plow blades and salt loads will have gotten there first.

I've done my share of slipping and sliding, even going into the ditch once to the delight of two 14-year-old girls in the back seat. So I'm very cautious now, even if the road has been plowed and salted – and it usually is. It's such a relief to make it to the bridge safely whenever I creep down Blair Road. But then I have to go up the opposite hill; I've learned where to speed up so my car won't stall. There may be fishtailing and spinning tires, but I make it every time.

Today the trip down Blair Road is relatively easy. Salt has started to melt the snow leaving only slippery slush to navigate. Even so, the car behind me hurries around when I pull off the road at the bridge to get my photos – probably relieved not to be following my so-very-cautious driving.

The next time I see the Grand River is from the passenger's side of our car on my way home from the hospital on Wednesday, January 26, around noon. Although my camera is in the car, I decide not to ask Colby to stop. We had a weekend storm – twelve inches of snow, temperatures in the single-digits. Good time to be in a warm hospital, if one can call having one's knee taken apart and bionic parts installed a good time. My view out the hospital window was obstructed by fixed mini-blinds. All I could tell was that everything outside was white.

I scan the river as we drive across the bridge. It is frozen except for a few disconnected open areas of water about two to six feet wide in the middle. This week should finish the freezing – temperatures are not predicted to rise. The TV reports that Lake Erie is also almost frozen solid.

I don't know when I'll be able to come to the bridge again. A lot depends on my recovery, but I'll be thinking about its silent run under the ice this week. Noisy water will return when the weather warms – just as I will as soon as my knee heals.

38 IT'S FROZEN

Thursday, February 3, 11:30 a.m., 33° F.

This is the first cloudy day in seven days. And even though daily sunshine melts some snow, five inches still remain on the ground. I want to see how much ice cover is on the Grand River. Colby drives me to the doctor's office in Madison to have the staples in my left knee incision removed. I become the driver upon leaving. Colby will be away on business next week and I will need to drive myself to outpatient physical therapy. Because it's my left knee and an automatic shift car, I am able to get my stiff leg inside if the car seat is pushed all the way back. Off to Painesville I drive so we can return library books, do some banking at the drive-up window, and fill up the gas tank.

Descending Blair Road from the north, I strain to see the river. All the land is snow-covered highlighting the dark green eastern hemlocks climbing the bluffs. Bare tree trunks punctuate the continuous white, most of them brown and gray except for the cream tones of my favorite sycamore tree with its three large trunks commanding attention.

This road and bridge were named after Robert Blair, a Scotsman who moved to Ohio from Massachusetts after the War of 1812. A businessman, he noticed bog ore was being hauled overland for forging south of Chardon – about fifteen miles from the Grand River and even farther from the source of the bog ore north in Madison. In 1825 he built a new blast furnace for the Geauga Iron Company near the Grand River on the northwest flatland. A coal shed for charcoal was placed near his homestead at the top of the north hill. Two railroad tracks connected the shed to the furnace; a coal-laden car would descend to the river while an empty one ascended. It's unclear if the existing road and bridge are at the site of the furnace since the river crossing used to be farther east. However his legacy lives on in the naming that occurred.

We are at the bridge. The Grand River is frozen completely – no open water anywhere. So now I know – the Grand River can and does freeze over completely in the winter. A flat plate of ice covers the water channel with occasional piles of smaller chunks here and there. Perhaps some ice was fractured yesterday when the temperature rose only to refreeze overnight. Lake Erie is usually completely ice-covered by the second week of February with more than half of the ice one to two feet thick. (An article in *The Plain Dealer*, March 23, 2009, reports that winter ice cover in the middle of Lake Erie has declined 30% since the 1970s, but natural variability is at least as large a factor as global and regional climate change. Confusing, yes, but the article concludes that global warming is happening.)

I try to visualize the volume and force of water moving downstream under the river's ice crown. It's been one of the top four snowiest Januarys on record. Lowering the car window, I listen as my husband runs from side to side taking photos per my instructions. I hear some wind in the trees but the river runs silently. Downstream the smooth center of the river looks like a great ice skating rink. Even the freshets falling off the south bluff have frozen in place. It's a bleak, cold winter day. I'd love to be the one taking the photos, but I'm not dumb enough to chance a healing new steel knee with less than full extension on crutches at the snow piles. On our way home, Colby remarks that the ice cover won't break up until a rain storm swells the water and lifts the ice up. Huh? That doesn't make sense to me but I've had enough time away from my bed and am too tired to argue. This coming week may change the river scene entirely. Temperatures are predicted to hit 51° F. by Monday or Tuesday. It may be quite a production for me to get photos next week with my walker or cane. Just like the Grand River, I'll have to wait and see what time will bring.

39 THE BREAK-UP

Monday, February 14, 11:00 a.m., 48° F.

I missed the ice break-up. I didn't have the nerve to ask Colby to do one more thing on the weekend. He has graciously taken over my chores – filling the bird feeders, watering plants, collecting the trash, emptying the compost pail – while I recover from my total knee replacement. And he had to go to Florida today for work, so I did not get to the Grand River when the warm spell and rain arrived.

Today after seeing the dentist, I decide to go home and rest before my physical therapy session in three hours. I tire easily still. I'm also anxious about the impending physical therapy since the at-home exercises haven't made much difference in how far I can bend my knee. Perhaps I should have been more vigorous, but I don't like pain. I have been able to switch from the walker to a cane indoors though.

I drive past my usual parking place and stop closer to the bridge, not caring if the car overlaps the roadway. Pushing my seat back as far as it will go, I swing my left leg out the open door and follow it with my right leg and cane. I look and listen thoroughly for traffic since my ambulation will be slow. I manage to get to my east photo position and hook my cane on the guardrail before three vehicles cross the bridge.

I take my time looking around on this Valentine's Day. The river has completely thawed and flows fully, its muddy water stretching over some of its banks. Along the banks and in the flood zones are piles of ice slabs about eight inches thick – some as big as coffee tables, others gameboard size. I suspect when the ice broke, these pieces were forced onto the land by the rising, rushing water. And yes, Colby, it was after a rain. I doubt the river will freeze solid again this year, but you never know; it's only the middle of February.

Although the sky is overcast, there is enough light to effect the river's color. Upstream the river is silver and so reflective I can barely make out the undulating minute surface waves. Directly below me, muddy brown underlies the rippling water disappearing under the bridge. Downstream the Grand River starts out somewhat reflective but ends up opaque black as it bends out of sight. Some snow cover remains on the banks there. The above-freezing temperature is welcome today.

I manage to limp my way back to the car after taking my photos. Reversing my leg swings, I travel home only to do the leg swinging maneuvers one more time. The temperature continues to rise during the day. The air feels spring-like, and Emmett wants in and out the back door several times – even at my bedtime. By then I am tired of getting up and down with my cane to open and close the door for him. I quit, and he gives up, falling asleep on my temporary bed that Colby fashioned out of some two-by-fours and a spare twin mattress. The dining room windows next to the bed are not curtained so even at night when I wake up to take another pain pill or struggle to the bathroom, I can see Rana Pond and the woods beyond in the varying darkness.

Two days later, the temperature plummets. I awake on Wednesday to three inches of snow and a winter wonderland again. If it weren't such a production, I would go to the Grand River again. But I will be out soon enough for another physical therapy session. I have a job to do here – recuperation. The river will continue its work in February's cold air.

40 FLOES AND THERAPY

Thursday, February 24, 11:15 a.m., 20° F.

This is the first time since I started this project that I lack enthusiasm for my visit to the Grand River. Although I've seen the river twice already this week going to and from physical therapy, I've grown listless and weary during my recovery, and have been avoiding the effort it takes to get out of the car for photos. On Tuesday I could have gotten a terrific photo because the sun highlighting the eastern half of the water and valley was also sparkling off the snow-covered high bluff and trees. But I didn't have my camera and the last batch of developed photos had a red overcast – not from the weather. I hope it was a defective roll of film and not my camera because I've already completed four weeks' worth of photos on the next roll.

I'm also on the downward leg of this project and realize it will be drawing to a close in approximately 17 weeks. I plan to move on to something else but hope I can count on the Grand River not to change much. So far, any changes I have noticed have been subtle. Today I note that my log perch has rotated because now a branch is sticking straight up that used to reach for the river. Also the log benchmark on the other side is now almost parallel with the bank. Evidently it has moved too. And there is a new tree trunk closer to the bridge on the east side blocking the footpath that boaters and fishermen use to get down to the river.

Changes have occurred, and I wonder what the spring rains will bring. Colder weather these past few days has brought ice plates back on the inward aspects of the river's curves and little pancake floes to the main current, but there should not be any big changes in this channel unless the 'big one' occurs along the New Madrid fault. Or a meteor hits northeast Ohio. Or it rains forty days and forty nights. Or the two remaining dams are removed.

The Harpersfield Dam is deteriorating and discussion has started about what to do. There's a lot of silt built up behind the concrete bulkhead, but the river would manage that just like it does the ebbs and flows of its seasonal volumes. Right now the dam prevents the sea lamprey from going farther upstream – another consequence to consider. An invasive eel-like species, lampreys got into the Great Lakes through Atlantic shipping canals in the 1920s and have threatened native fish since. And the dam is a scenic draw for recreation, fishing, and tourists. Currently there is no money to do anything about it either way. Let's see if nature will have a say.

I love knowing the river continues steadfastly on even though I may not be watching it as closely as before. I'm glad I finally stopped today to get my photos. Looking at the river's leisurely flow with pancake ice patches between the snow shrouded banks rekindles my interest. I feel calmed and remotivated.

On the next day, on my way home from physical therapy, I'm struck anew by the beauty of the valley at the Blair Road Bridge. Snow clings to all ground surfaces, the south bluff looks like a many layered cake with prickly decorations on top and runny frosting at its base, and chunks of ice now whitened by fresh snowfall clutter the riverside trees. Even though the sky is overcast, there is enough sunlight to create faint shadows on the land and river. Stopping at the beginning of the bridge, I lower my car's front windows and snap a couple photos. My rule to always take my photos at the same three locations seems too restrictive today.

I find myself attracted to things that aren't perfect. The two story deck at the back of my house was left to weather naturally. One railing section is bowed slightly concave. Here and there sections have pulled back from a post or a post-top has split, its crack running for the ground twelve feet below. One post, obeying an internal twist, long ago moved off square and now adjoining boards fight their nails – the nails are losing. It's as if some spirit of the tree from which this wood was cut still lives on my balcony, making itself known by twisting out of shape what the lumberyard worker and carpenter strove to straighten. "Look what happened here," I say to visitors.

Likewise the Grand River calls me again to see what is happening there – the subtle everyday changes that may be missed unless one is looking.

41 CHORES AND MAGIC

Thursday, March 3, 1:30 p.m., 34° F.

A foot of snow fell over the weekend; the temperatures stayed below freezing until today. It's unseasonably cold weather, and the Grand River is surrounded by an opaque snow blanket. Ice shelves have formed on the bank curves where the current is less, and pancake-sized ice floes are once again running the river. If this cold keeps up and the river freezes solid again (highly unlikely), I may get a chance to see the ice breakup that I missed before. But it's too close to spring and any cold spells probably won't last long enough to freeze the whole surface. I missed it this year.

Most everything is black and white in the gray light. One patch of blue sky hovers over the north bluff. Reflections of bare tree trunks at the bridge and dark green eastern hemlocks at the western bend look like landscape paintings from an art gallery. The river flows gently and quietly within its ice shrouded banks.

Two cars go by as I lean my cane against the guardrail and snap my photos. There's an icon flashing on the camera's instruction window, and I don't know what it means. Have I damaged another roll of film and lost my photos for the past five weeks? I already have many photos of snow and ice at the bridge; however, each week looks different to me. Perhaps only I will appreciate the nuances between the winter photos.

I am such a bag of contradictions. Last week I was writing about enjoying failings, but this week I feel annoyed because my project plan may have gone awry. I dreamt up this project, visualizing a perfect completion in spite of the knowledge that life never goes smoothly. Some discoveries are pleasant, like the goats, the bell tower chimes, the river's music; others are annoying or sad like the potentially lost photos, the graffiti, and the huge hollow in the sycamore tree. I was surprised today that last week's visit felt like such a chore.

I am reminded of doing chores in winter as a child. I would reluctantly get ready to leave the warm farmhouse. It seemed to take forever to get bundled up – to struggle into coat, boots, hat and gloves. I got so hot doing it that stepping out into the cold was a relief, but by the time I got to the barn with the egg basket or milk buckets, I appreciated all the apparel. And then being around the cows or handling hay and straw bales was enough to make me unzip my coat. I was prepared to just get through the jobs, but invariably I returned gladdened by something – the warm flanks of the stanchioned cows, the silky feathers of the chickens I cautiously lifted to search for eggs, the smell of the teat-released milk in the metal bucket as I poured it through the strainer, or the sharp inhalations needed when the errant wind found my face. I felt rewarded for my effort and superior to persons who did not venture out in such weather. I tried to get my sister, who didn't have any outside chores, to listen to my descriptions of how I braved the bad weather, but she never showed an adequate amount of interest to satisfy me. Nothing like a little fresh air, huh?

Similarly, at the Grand River I always feel rewarded if I step out of my car to stand along the Blair Road Bridge's rails and observe the water below and the valley beyond. It's a magical location to me; I claim ownership just because I spend the time.

My home is another magical spot for me – for numerous reasons. Today I was reminded of one of them. Twenty-five feet behind my house starts a second-growth forest on my five and a half acres that blends seamlessly into the Hell Hollow Wilderness Area. The wind today crescendoed as it howled through the forest before slamming into my home's wood frame and swooping over the roof. Shake, rattle and roll.

On my way home Friday afternoon, I have to slow on the Blair Road Bridge because in front of me a red car with two passengers is creeping over the bridge. It makes me smile to see two heads pivoting right and left to see the beautiful and magical Grand River before the car picks up speed for the hill ahead. I am so glad that the valley almost stopped them; I know that pull. Hopefully, they will be back just as I will, and the next time maybe they will get out of their car for the full sight and sound of the river.

42 NESTS AND DAMS

Wednesday, March 9, 1:30 p.m., 21° F.

The river is full; its gurgling muddy waters have risen up to my log markers on both sides of the channel. Any ice still left after Monday's melt (it got up to 52° F.) are just jumbled piles in the slower waters along the curves. Shades of gray, brown, and black contrast with some white along the banks where the deeper snows still cling to the soil. The gray cloudy sky admits a hint of sunlight if you look hard enough through the snowflakes blown fiercely by the strong cold wind.

I struggle to the guardrail while trying to shield my camera from the snowflakes. The last time I took photos when it was snowing, there were water spots on the prints. (I did not lose my photos from the last few weeks and now have a new roll of film in the camera). I take my usual three photos and then for good measure snap one more from inside the car after drying the lens. In the distance the storm morphs into a white haze. I notice some new debris on the downstream side of the bridge – a large log that has collected other branches on its upstream side. I like the deeper tones the river makes when its water hits the bridge's stanchion. How I love it when I am all alone with the river. But it is cold, so I rush – as fast as one can rush while limping – back to my car and head uphill.

On Ford Road at the top of the hill, a lone Canada goose glides across the road in front of me, its downward-curving wings aiding its way to a field on my right. It reminds me that on Monday I had seen three Canada geese on the Grand River when I crossed the bridge. One was perched on an ice floe about ten feet into the channel and the other two were on the bank. Since they mate for life, it was probably a family unit which remains together through winter until they return to their breeding grounds. The female builds a nest out of sticks, grass, weeds, and moss before lining it with down. The site is usually slightly elevated dry ground near water. Well, that almost fits for here right now but just wait until all this snow melts and the spring rains come. I hope experience has taught her to build back from the banks. Incubation of four to seven white eggs takes 25-30 days. On past spring canoe trips, I have seen goslings whose parents would advance toward us while loudly honk-a-honking.

Below Paine Falls, I've seen several beaver dams built in the fall only to be swept away in spring. I suspect the river at the Blair Road Bridge is not desirable for beavers either, but they are present upstream on the lowland portion of the Grand River. This is a great thing. American Indians called the beaver the "sacred center" of the land. By creating wetlands with their dams, they help feed other mammals, fishes, turtles, frogs, birds and ducks. They also slow the flows of floodwaters, prevent erosion, raise the water table, and purify water by breaking down toxins, such as pesticides. You couldn't ask more of one species. They almost became extinct in the early 1900s due to trapping and the draining of wetlands for agriculture. Current populations are as low as five percent of those present prior to European settlement. They breed only once a year alongside streams, impacting only a small percentage of the landscape. At two years of age, the kits leave home in spring to find their own places. I wonder if the destroyed dams I viewed were the youngsters' first attempts at homemaking.

The closer I get to my house, the heavier the snowfall. Over the next thirty minutes it's a whiteout from a lake-effect storm, and the ground is once again white. If I had stayed just thirty minutes longer at the bridge, my photos would have been entirely different. This is when I have to fight my desire to capture every changing moment; instead I'll just obsess for a few moments on what I missed.

Now sunlight appears although the strong northwest winds continue unabated. Cold and more snow are forecast for the weekend. I am finally joining the crowd of complainers about all the cold and snow. Now that it's March, it would be nice to have a hint of spring. I do believe the birds are singing more, and Colby spied a red-winged blackbird at the backyard feeders. A great comfort is the longer daylight.

I am looking forward to the greening of the Grand River valley. Once it's warmer, I'll be able to spend another hour by its banks. My left knee should have full range of motion by then. I'm already discarding my cane on most of my indoor walking and I have a trekking pole to use outside.

Sunlight reaches my computer keys, but the view outside is still white, gray, and brown except for the one cardinal resting in the serviceberry tree. Emmett sleeps in his favorite chair while several miles away the sonorous Grand River flows in the cold sunlit air.

43 SHORT SPANS

Monday, March 14, 10:30 a.m., 25° F.

It was 12° F. when I got up this morning around 8 a.m. Fortunately for me the temperature, although still below freezing, has risen thirteen degrees by the time I arrive at the Blair Road Bridge. It does not feel like winter; it feels like spring. The air seems softer as a hot sun shines brightly overhead and sparkles off the water.

And the water seems different. Is it because I feel that spring is just around the corner, or has there been a noticeable turn in the river's animus? The water has receded from the banks on the slow side of the curves, and gravel beds are visible again. On the east side there is a small rapid, as if the river wants to be merry and help spring along. In reality, the volume of water is lower, and the rocks beneath are disturbing the flow. The river still sounds deep, and large snowflake-covered ice floes swish swiftly downstream. Some plate ice clings to the banks, especially in the eddy right before the bridge's stacked stone embankment.

I stand and stare for many minutes breathing in the cold air, my sense of balance disturbed by the fast flowing water when I look directly down. I have to glance farther downstream to restore my equilibrium. I am struck by the height of the valley walls and think of the millions of years it took to form what I see in front of me. I am jealous of that time. Assuming humans are the most sentient beings so far, why is our time so short? A little bit of self-importance there, huh? We do outlive all species except the Galapagos tortoise, box turtle, and carp, which all average life spans of over 100 years. Gray whales live seventy years, which is close to the human species' average-expected eighty years. Unfortunately, humans do a lot more harm during their lives than do the gray whales. So much for the preciousness of sentience. And why does it take so long to learn how to be in the now?

Reluctantly, I return to my car and drive up the north hill. Three-quarters of the way up, I notice the sun is highlighting the east side of the bell tower on the south ridge. It's time to try for some photos of the tower using my small zoom lens. I love thinking of the surprise first-time drivers on Blair Road get when the chimes sound.

"What was that? Did you just hear bells? Must be a church in Painesville, but you wouldn't think you could hear them all the way out here."

I wonder how long the tower will stand and its bells chime above the river. I hope the owner has made plans for the tower to ring in perpetuity. Speaking of perpetuity, I was heartened by an article in *The Plain Dealer* today about the preservation of three farms in our county using a combination of federal, state and county monies. If it were up to me, I would go around preserving lots of land. When I dream about winning the Ohio Super Lotto, I also fantasize about using some of the money to buy up scenic spaces in my county. Although I have my small place in the country and am grateful for the privilege of living there, I cringe when I see woods cleared or fields divided for houses. Since I moved on my country road 17 years ago, there have been 12 new homes built, streetlights placed at each road intersection, lines painted down the pavement, and roadside traffic signs proliferating like the orange lilies brought over by the pioneers. I miss the less encumbered land and road scenes.

At least so far, the Grand River remains almost the same, flowing as ever over its riverbed, any changes so slow that I won't notice them in my lifetime. It's the ancient topography I love. In this day and age we are blessed with satellite images of the entire planet; it's amazing how detailed the final zooming shows the ground. I can start somewhere over Ohio on my computer and zoom in on the trail of the Grand River through Lake County as it meanders to Lake Erie. Pulling back on the screen, I can follow the flow of water to the Atlantic Ocean, whereupon I realize my insignificance again. That's why I want to pay attention every day to the weather, to the forest, to the river. They will continue for eons. By being aware I boldly claim a speck of immortality for one instant.

44 THE BELL TOWER

Monday, March 21, 10:30 a.m., 37° F.

It is still cold, but the snow has melted except for isolated patches where shade was dominant. At the Grand River, the water is free of ice, but thick slabs on the banks and flood zone linger, unfazed by one day of sunlight over the weekend. The high and rushing coffee-with-cream river fills its channel and flows over the low grasses up to my north-side log perch. On the high south bluff downstream, freshets remain frozen ice cream cones – pure white against the damp-darkened soil and deep green eastern hemlocks lined across the face and rim of the bluff. Even though the temperature is above freezing, it feels cold and bleak on this second day of spring. Enough already; it's time for some warmth. Back home tulip and daffodil leaves have pierced the soil. But where is daily sunlight, and where is the fresh air?

The Grand River feels ancient and old today. The Tudor house along its banks looks tired and grungy. It's a day of repetition – same road, same river, same job, and same cloudy sky. I look around for something fresh to see. Ahead over the bridge there is a car parked halfway up the north hill. Someone is fishing today? Out somewhere in the frigid, forceful waters of the river in hip-high boots casting for steelhead trout? So change is afoot after all.

I think of my home and the fleeting time I will be its caretaker. Why does it matter so much to complete the new flower bed at the wood's edge? When I walk my property, I see large chunks of broken cement from a barn embankment that used to be south of my driveway – the only reminder of the farm that once flourished here. Grasses, wild rose bushes and struggling sumac trees almost obscure the debris now. I like wondering about the people who hunted in my woods or farmed the fields now reforested. What about the future? Will the Grand River fare as well in the future? Or will it be sacrificed to human greed? Can its banks be kept free of development? Will its water remain as clean?

I'm hoping my pessimism is a reflection of dealing with the end of winter and not a persistent state. I am usually optimistic and encouraged daily by good news in the paper or a discovery or invention announced over the radio. In general, I feel the human species is steadily, albeit with ups and downs, becoming a better steward of our planet.

For my immediate surroundings and my favorite river, I place my faith in the Grand River Partners and the Ohio Department of Natural Resources. I place my faith in individuals who think their existence has more meaning when they care for their environs, when they finish the new flower bed, paint over graffiti or pick up litter. But mostly I place my faith in the magnetism of the mighty river.

So I proceed with my plans to get more information about the bell tower. Requesting a visit and interview through the Ohio Nature Conservancy hasn't worked. I call the local newspaper, *The News-Herald,* and ask to use its archives, because I recall reading an article about the tower after my move to this county in 1974. The subject index is too general to find the piece I recall. And the column could have been in the defunct *Telegraph* instead whose microfilm would take hours to scan. I have learned, however, from the *History of Leroy,* Second Edition, that the free-standing clock tower with its four bells is similar to one at the Oxford University of England. The carillon is a set of stationary bells, each producing one tone of the chromatic scale, and/or the melody played on such bells. (I craft a brief letter and drop it in the mailbox at Walden II on March 30, 2008 but never receive a response.) Meanwhile, the Grand River with its full load of impenetrable muddy water passes continuously by the bluff where the bells chime on the quarter hour.

45 THE BELL SISTERS

May 9, 2007

The Bell sisters, who live in the white clapboard farmhouse on top the south bluff above the Blair Road Bridge, said yes to my mailbox request for an interview. It's the oldest inhabited property overlooking the valley. I like its layout – a small white house connected to a similar-sized brown barn by a vine-covered breezeway. Behind the house are a few outbuildings; one, the classic red of Ohio's barns, has an idle greenhouse attached. All is well tended and neat.

As I park behind their garage, its door glides up. I am welcomed by Virginia Bell who leads me inside through crowded rooms to meet her bed-bound sister, Audrey. The third and youngest sister, Jean, died a few years ago.

Although the sisters say they may not have much to tell me, we converse for an hour. All three of them were physical education teachers who never married and lived here for the past 35 years except for wintering in Florida. Initially, the farm was only a summer home purchased by a grandfather who deeded it to their parents. In 1976, the sisters moved here permanently. All three retired from teaching or school administration by 1978.

At age 82 and 84, the bonds between Audrey and Virginia are warm and supportive. Memories are shared freely and laughter comes easily. Their pride of family, place and achievement is obvious. I like their soft faces, sweet eyes, and refined voices. They were glad Jean was a girl; glad there were no brothers.

They recount childhood walks on the then-graveled Blair Road to the 'crow's nest' – a wooden platform their parents had built out over the water. The property then included all the land from their buildings to the river. Their parents would sit and read the newspaper or go fishing. The sisters would talk, go swimming, or sit on the covered bridge and wait for cars to drive by.

Jean saved Audrey's life once when a canoe they had dug out of the riverbank broke up about three bends downstream and Audrey started floating away. In the spring they would run any rapids in a plastic boat; jumping fish sometimes joined them. Turtle soup was a favorite. And they remember encounters with leeches in the stiller, shallower water.

At first they were upset when the covered bridge was torn down and replaced by a metal one in 1956. But on second thought, it eliminated more traffic – people coming to cross the last covered bridge in Lake County. Virginia takes me around the house to see the framed needlepoint of the covered bridge and aerial photographs of the bridge and their farm. The walls of all the rooms I get to see are covered with photographic memories of family and place.

The bell tower is another story. I find it delicious that the Bell sisters reside next to the property with the bell tower, but they want to shoot the bells. It destroys the peace and quiet of the valley for them. "At least the churches in town only ring their bells on Sundays," one sister says. While I love hearing the bells, I'm not living on the rim of the valley where every chime is heard on the hour and quarter hour during daylight. So something seemingly romantic has another side – I love it that the Bell sisters hate the bells.

At one point car races were proposed for Blair Road. However, the organizer's wife wouldn't go across the covered bridge, so the formal racing never happened. They have seen many a Mad Hatter's Canoe Race though, which used to come all the way past the bridge.

They speak highly of the people who occupy the home below them; they sold that parcel to them. I remember how disappointed I was to see a house and tennis courts where previously woods and wetland existed. "You should see the house; it's wonderful," one sister says. I am reluctant to see it or meet the occupants. I prefer to dislike the change and refuse to have my mind changed by nice people.

The Bell sisters have no immediate heirs; their property will probably be sold after their deaths. (Audrey died in 2011, Virginia moved to a condominium in town. Their property has sold – children's toys are lying about.)

I ask to walk to the valley's rim behind the house when the interview is concluded. One of their helpers takes me past the backyard pond visible from Audrey's bedside window where I am warned not to go near the swan. A trail leads through sixty feet of mature trees to the edge of the valley. In either direction one sees the Grand River and its bends. Far below on the right and tucked up against the south bluff is the Blair Road Bridge. This view is not visible from the house; only the void between the forested hills hints of the river valley's chasm.

The sisters often think about the Grand River but rarely get to see it now except when out in their car. They were right. Nothing major happened in their years here, and isn't that wonderful? I'm glad I got to meet them. I'm glad they get to live here. I'll watch for the afterimage of three girls frolicking in the water whenever I cross the Blair Road Bridge over the Grand River. Let's hope the bells don't ring at the same time.

46 RIVER SONGS

Thursday, March 31, 3:30 p.m., 52° F.

At last some warmth has arrived. The sun has been shining more over the past few days. Every bit of snow is gone. The heat is a delight; every time I step outside, I feel lighter. Today I only needed my purple sweater while outside.

When I arrive at the Grand River, I notice even the ice slabs are gone. The water level is down, and I see how dark brown the underlying vegetation on the banks has become over the winter. A low-grade rapid has a soft ruffling sound. When I stand at the bridge's west guardrail, the sparkling water makes me squint. The gusting northwest winds create such ripples that it appears the river is flowing upstream. I hope the strong light won't bleach my photos of this beautiful scene.

I think about canoeing the river. But it's only dreaming – these waters are too cold for anybody except for hardy fishermen in hip-waders. I often see them whenever I cross the Grand River on one of the roads in and out of Painesville.

I think about sitting for an hour at the side of the river again, but my tree trunk seat looks wet and the banks are spongy and muddy. And a few more weeks of recovery time for my left knee would be wise before venturing on uneven terrain. I'm not able to bend it fully yet. My struggles up and down stairs make me feel so old.

My timing is off. I haven't heard the bell tower chiming on any of my past visits. But that's okay. It's been a great day off from work with every appointment and errand executed perfectly from my doctors' visits to renewing my driver's license before enduring an hour of physical therapy. And now I stand by the river where the water continually flows. Its music reminds me that songs have been written about this river.

Saturday evening my husband and I went to the Taverne of Perry to hear Alex Bevan perform. A Northeast Ohio regional star since he started performing in 1968, he is best known locally for his song, "Skinny Little Boy (From Cleveland, Ohio)" wherein he's "come to chase your women and drink your beer." A singer/songwriter who just kept after his craft, his music has evolved and matured. Most recently, he accepted an EMMY for his post score of NBC's American Promise documentary segment "The Rustbelt Blues."

I have admired and enjoyed his songs about rivers and Lake Erie for many years. His "Grand River Lullaby," while a human love song, rewards the listener with its attention to the river: "I want to take you/ where the water winds/ make love beneath the pines/ hold you forever

beneath the starry skies/ I'll sing for you Grand River lullabies."
Although his "Middle Fork" is about an Idaho river, its description of
seeing, hearing, and experiencing a river always stirs me, and it has the
best chorus, which I also apply to the Grand River although its name
wouldn't rhyme: "Those who run the Middle Fork/ don't give a damn
about New York/ the river's making music/ that Broadway'll never
know." And finally, there's the chorus from "Copper River Float" that
applies to any river anywhere: "I want to spend my days on the river/ I
want to spend my nights out there too/ I want to spend my days on the
river/ you can come along if you choose." He signs off his emails with
"See you down river."

As much as I enjoy hearing these songs, it doesn't equal for me
the music found riverside as wind flows through the flood zone trees,
birds sing in the valley air, and the water sings softly today.

47 SPRING SNOWSTORM

Tuesday, April 5, 5 p.m., 70° F.

It was the most spectacular spring snowfall I have ever witnessed. The storm started overnight on Friday and continually dumped wet, heavy stuff until Sunday afternoon. Our electricity went off at midnight Saturday (I heard the computer power-backup beeping) and was not restored until 6 p.m. on Sunday. Thank goodness for my engineer husband who in 2001 bought one of the surplus generators left over from the millennium scare. It permits us to have the well pump, refrigerator, hot water heater or baseboard heaters on at different times so that some of the comforts of home are still available. Unfortunately or fortunately, the cable TV service was also out. So I finished reading the sixth Harry Potter book and started a new one about mountain lions returning to Michigan while opening the back door off and on for Emmett, who thought he wanted to go outside until confronted with the thick blowing snow. The snowiest winter record at Cleveland Hopkins Airport – 104 plus inches – was broken. Just talk to any stalwart soul in the snowbelt for the real skinny – the total snowfall was a lot more than that.

Monday dawned with a warming spell, up to fifty degrees, and all the snow began to melt. I took some photos of the high and rushing Grand River on my way to work. I thought that would be my recorded visit this week, but on my way home today I think about all the snow that no doubt has melted in the seventy-degree day and eagerly drive to the river.

The coffee-with-cream colored river has overflowed its banks and is swirling around the tree trunks on the flood zone. Its torrent over buried stones and past the Blair Road Bridge abutments is creating rolling, sloshing rapids. I take my usual three photos, hoping the sun highlighting the water doesn't pale the downstream shot. I walk the bridge, hugging the rails on both sides for some direct shots into the water. I just can't stop taking photos. The flow is hypnotizing, the sound is soothing; my sunglasses temper the piercing sparkles.

It's spring, and this day is rapidly wiping away the snowiest winter ever recorded. I don't wear a coat, warm breezes tease my hair, and hot sun rays strike my bare arms. Multiple cars and trucks pass me as I ponder the water. I'm here at a time when people are going home from their daytime labors. I pay them no mind except to squeeze my body tighter against the bridge railing as they drive by.

A voice behind me calls, "Are you going to jump?" I turn to see a sheriff's car with a deputy in the driver's seat. He must have driven slowly onto the bridge because I didn't hear his approach. It saddens me to think that law enforcement officers have to consider the worst that could happen instead of assuming that someone is just enjoying the view. I feel the pull of the water today, the disorientation created by the swift flow under a stationary bridge. One could end his/her life with a leap into these fierce currents even from this fourteen foot high bridge.

I am reminded of the time crossing the high State Route 528 Bridge upstream when I saw three persons rush from their parked cars toward a man at the left side railing. They reached him and were hugging his body as I slowly drove by. I didn't stop – there were enough people already there. I felt so proud of the ones who stopped to thwart the leap. Next day the suicide attempt was confirmed by a newspaper item that reported the man was now in a psychiatric facility.

I recall another newspaper article several years ago about a man driving south who witnessed a young man run across the width of that bridge and leap without hesitation over the west railing. I can only imagine how shocked the driver was. I bet no one survives the 200 foot fall off there.

It's been a struggle to find any information on suicides at the State Route 528 high-level bridge. The woman answering the phone at the Madison Police Department remembers that a woman jumped off the bridge shortly after its dedication in 1962. The Madison Fire Chief (employed 20 years) remembers an incident somewhere around Christmas in 1989-1991. All the firefighters were at a holiday party when a man jumped. He survived the fall, but is now a quadriplegic. The fire chief recalls the medical helicopter waving itself off when approaching the bridge, choosing not to fly into the river valley with its own microclimate of up-and-down drafts.

Although there were 36 suicides listed as such in 2004 for all of Lake County, to find the official reports is a task I don't wish to pursue. In addition, when a body is found at the base of a bridge, how can one know if it was suicide or the person was pushed or slipped? My curiosity has been sated by this small amount of sad information.

Interestingly, the fences added to the State Route 528 Bridge that I thought were to prevent suicides are for stopping cars and/or debris from falling over the knee-high concrete walls after accidents. They seem to have stopped the suicides too since neither of my contacts can recall any incidents since the eight foot high wire mesh tops were added. I think the green screens are ugly and I miss the more open views I once had of the unexpected valley on this seemingly flat land. However, if they prevent another suicide, that's good. Maybe if some vines, like native bittersweet, were started at all four ends and allowed to creep along toward the center of the bridge, there would be greenery and small white flowers in the spring with gorgeous orange berries all winter long, just when color is needed. Since the river can't be seen from your car on this bridge, foliage would soften the hard lines of the screens.

In response to the deputy's question at the Blair Road Bridge, I laugh and say, "No, I just came to see the river. Isn't it great today?"

"Yeah, the Seeley Road Bridge is already flooded." (Seeley Road Bridge spans Paine Creek in Indian Point Metropark downstream about a mile before that tributary joins the Grand River.)

"Vrooman Road is next," he says.

"There's still a lot of snow up on the high ground," I say.

"I know. Ashtabula County still has lots too. The river's going to get higher. Be careful," he calls as he drives away.

Ashtabula County? I had momentarily forgotten the reach of the Grand River. The water I am now viewing mingles all the snowmelt from five counties. The ancient riverbed with its recirculating moisture and movement is interwoven with the past, present, and future of northeast Ohio. Again I realize how I am but an instance on this day and dispensable to its history. But all I have is now, and this now is filled with mighty, muddy water that stretches from the shale bluffs onto the flood zone while roaring its passage through this valley.

. 48 SAND AND CLAY

Tuesday, April 12, 12:30 p.m., 48° F.

It's been sunny and clear all week; the blue skies and sunlight are so welcome. So far there haven't been any April showers – it's as if last week's huge spring snowstorm coalesced all the moisture into one weekend. The river responded and only flooded Seeley and Vrooman roads.

At the Blair Road Bridge, the river has receded into its channel. I scan for signs of the prior high water and see on the southwest shale bluff an obvious change in the soil's color four feet up from the water. Other undetectable changes may have happened – all part of a millennium's worth of geology. I like the lower, gentler water as the riverbed rocks form rapids that sing their own songs – sounds that I would love to hear from my bedroom. I wonder if Slender Man and Slender Woman have thrown open their bedroom window yet this season.

While welcome, this weather of warmer days and cool nights makes me impatient. April is a hard month to wait out. At my house red and yellow bud swellings on some trees are unfolding into leaves. I cut daffodils for a table bouquet; the citrus aroma permeates the house. One lone blooming pink hyacinth stands guard by the garage door. Much as I would like its heady perfume inside my house, I won't cut it and return that corner to only brown tones.

The river's browns are lighter – its water looking like tea-without-milk but still opaque. As the banks dry out, some new grass blades are pushing through last year's flattened, dead growth. Soil is being carried out to Lake Erie where the winter ice has not melted completely. That explains the cold winds. Northeast Ohio stays cooler longer in the spring but warmer longer in the fall than inland – all because of the large body of water to the north.

Many frosts and perhaps more snow will come our way before Memorial Day when at last it will be safe to start a garden. Only cold weather vegetables like peas and lettuce can be placed in the soil as soon as it is workable. I augment my gardens' clay soils every year with compost or topsoil, but still the ground clumps on my shovel even after Memorial Day.

I am jealous of people gardening north of the Grand River in my township. Although all of the land was once covered by glacial ice, we are now in different soil regions. I live in the Mahoning-Canfield-Rittman-Chili section (#6), a Major Land Resource Area designated as Northeastern Forage and Forest. Many areas that were once farmed are now urban or wooded. North of the river is the Lake States Fruit, Truck, and Dairy Region in the Conotton-Conneaut-Allis section (#2). Their soils were formed by glacial till and lake/beach sediments. And therein lies all the difference. I work so hard to get tillable garden soil, and they just have to dip their shovels into the land to get all that wonderful crumbly stuff that vegetables love.

So what a difference again the Grand River valley makes. I'll be watching the river and scanning the trees for spring's progress since I can't garden yet. The goats are still in their barn at the top of the north hill. I'm looking forward to their cavorting, but first some grass is needed.

49 WRITING WITH LIGHT

Tuesday, April 19, 5:05 p.m., 78° F.

It's an incredibly warm spring day. I'm returning home after picking up my car from Lou's Tire Mart. To my delight I was right about its misalignment. Colby thought the problem was created by our sloping roads.

I park at my usual place and notice how high the sun still is. Longer daylight allows me to see the Grand River at full sparkle today. The brown, heretofore flooded banks are turning green. Trees sprout little leaves – pale green and yellow canopy jewels. Still air intensifies the sun's rays – time for some Vitamin D.

I stand observing the scene, hearing a rapid's faint babbling between cars and trucks swooshing over the bridge. The vehicles are going both directions – the way to and from home for folks living along River Road and in LeRoy Township. Interstate 90 crosses Lake County from west to east on a line mostly parallel with the shoreline of Lake Erie, although ten miles inland. I like the fact that there is only one freeway exit in LeRoy Township at Vrooman Road. In order to get home from there, I wind around an attention-grabbing circuitous route up and down hills and over two bridges before entering a lovely half mile stretch of road with woods but no homes or power lines. My road, while straight for its entire one mile length, has a dip just before my driveway. I love all these twists and dips. Interstate roads might give us vistas, but there's nothing like a narrow, curved and hilly rural road to satisfy me. All this straightening for safety and speed takes away the adventure.

I take my three photos. As I'm returning to my car, a young man in a pick-up truck going up the south hill slows down and calls, "Are you stranded, ma'am?" "No, I'm fine, just taking pictures," I say and wave my camera. In hindsight I wish I would have said, "I'm fine, just writing with light," because that's what the word photography means. It was named by English astronomer John Herschel whose father discovered infrared.

Ma'am? What a quaint word! Here I was thinking that maybe men passing by were admiring my physique and casting a second look to check me out. This young man's words makes me feel my sixty years. Obviously I am changing more and faster than I care to note – I am not a river. I appreciate his good manners and concern though, maybe.

As I ease my car up the south hill, I peer through the trees and past the houses for another look at the river continually flowing east on this brilliant spring day. It looks deep enough for kayaking, but the water is still cold. Probably best to wait for May to go down the river.

50 ANOTHER SPRING SNOW

Monday, April 25, 11:15 a.m., 50° F.

The river is high again. Starting late Saturday night and continuing through Monday's early hours, another snowstorm hit northeast Ohio. Those of us at the higher elevations past the escarpment got thirteen to seventeen inches of that heavy wet snow that comes when temperatures hover around freezing. Everything was covered.

An acquaintance, who recently lost his wife, says: "Diane always remarked that the daffodils get bent down twice." My mother reported a neighbor's saying: "It snows three times after the forsythia blooms." I remember one spring when snow fell on the morning of May 19 but melted by the time a fundraising concert started that evening. Not that I desire a May snowfall. Two huge April snowstorms are enough.

Seventy-two percent of the time we have snow in April, averaging a total of three to four inches; however the largest total was set in 1957 – just over twenty-four inches. This year's nineteen inches does not beat that record, although this statistic is from the Cleveland Airport data center. And snow usually is rare after mid-April but not this year. The record for the snowiest winter ever (105 inches) had already been set by April 5th. This much more snow brings the total for the season to 117.9 inches, making it even harder to top. But in the snowbelt, the total was 157.58 inches! Even that did not top the record of 161.45 inches of snow in Chardon in 1959/1960. It's close enough for bragging rights. Bring on those grandchildren; have I got stories for them .

I drive slipping and sliding out of my snowy, slushy driveway. Colby, thinking winter was over, had already put the snow blower away in the shed. Thankfully the roads are clear. When I get to the Blair Road Bridge, there is very little snow to be seen. However, the water is up to the trees on all sides. All gravel beds are again covered, and the river, a churning beige giant, roars as it passes under the bridge.

When I approach the southeast abutment to take my first photo, I hear honking over the roar. Three Canada geese are squawking as they swim near the east bank. I hope they didn't have a nest on one of the gravel banks. Their honking stops when I retreat to the other side of the bridge. Just to confirm that they were honking at me, I cross back over the bridge, and their stay-away warnings begin again. As I finish my third photo on the west side, the bell tower chimes. The bells are muted by the river sounds, just faint tinkling in the distance.

After work, around 7:30 p.m., I encounter a mystery in progress when crossing the Grand River at the Main Street Bridge in Painesville. Two police cars with flashing lights are slowing traffic, and the Special

Rescue Unit from Fairport Harbor is turning into a parking lot across the road. What does Fairport Harbor (a small town north at the mouth of the Grand River on Lake Erie) have that Painesville doesn't? Divers! Two police officers are peering down into the shrubs at the northwest end of the bridge. Is there a body caught in the vegetation? The current is very swift here since the river comes around a seventy-five degree bend and slams into a high shale wall before the bridge. I know I shouldn't stop and add to the mess. I'll check the *News-Herald* tomorrow. When I relate my observations to Colby and my daughter later that night, neither of them think first of a body. I have been reading too many murder mysteries.

(The next day at work I learn that two males were canoeing down the river and got swept into the shrubs and debris on the southwest bank at the bridge and couldn't get out. I wonder who heard their hollers for help over the roar of the flood stage Grand River. No one was harmed in this ill-advised springtime lure to go down the river, but I bet they now know a thing or two about water hydraulics.)

On my way back down Blair Road, I see a man and a woman hiking along the road toward the bridge and another woman on the bridge as I cross it. The bridge woman has a smile on her face. I'm not the only one who comes to see the Grand River manage its load of water. Since my crossing this morning, the water now has spread farther into the woods past its first trees. I can hear the river's roaring even with my car windows closed. No snow anywhere.

Up the hill my car climbs to the plateau that includes my property, where six inches of snow remain, although patches of grass are seen here and there. Tomorrow should be even better at the Grand River. Temperatures are predicted in the 50s again. If the rains come, because what is April without showers, the Grand River will have even more water to handle.

51 BIRDS AND BIRDERS

Monday, May 2, 12:21 p.m., 40° F.

It's a cloudy and gray day. I am longing for warmer temperatures and some sunshine again, although I confess that too many days of clear skies wear me down. My SAD (seasonal affective disorder) is the reverse of Colby's experience. I need a cloudy day or at least intermittent shade now and again. To live permanently in sunny climes is not for me.

At the Grand River the water level has dropped since there has been no rain (or snow!) recently. The water flows inside the banks and white-tinged ripples are seen at the usual site of small rapids. In the quiet I hear their soft rustling.

What is that other noise coming from the north plateau? It sounds like a donkey's bray. There it goes again. I have never noticed a donkey anywhere up there, but the goats with four new kids are back out in the fenced pasture.

A lone Canada goose stands in the river – I hear another one honking farther east. All around me birds twitter although I don't see any in flight. The baleful sound of a train horn faintly blares in the west. And the bell tower sounds a few chimes.

It's high season for migratory birds here in northeast Ohio. There are lots of noted birding spots nearby along Lake Erie from Lakeshore Metropark in Perry, Headlands Beach next to the towns of Fairport Harbor and Grand River, the Mentor Marsh, and the electric company warmed waters in Eastlake. These and other IBAs (Important Bird Area) receive attention each week in Jim McCarty's birding column, *Aerial View*, in the Cleveland newspaper. I am happy to report that the Grand River environs is designated an IBA by the Ohio Audubon Society. Other specific sites also singled out: Grand River Wildlife Area (Trumbull County), Grand River Terraces (Ashtabula County), and the Mentor Marsh (Lake County).

Marietta, Ohio, is the birthplace of the magazine *Bird Watcher's Digest*, launched in 1978 from the living room of Bill Thompson, Jr., and his wife, Elsa. Their son, Bill Thompson III, is now the editor, and he wisely chose for his wife a writer named Julie Zickefoose. In addition to her frequent columns in the magazine, she draws and paints.

Ohio can claim at least two more famous birders as residents. One is Kenn Kaufman, most notably the author of *Kaufman Field Guide to Birds of North America.* The other is Larry Rosche, who first became known to me as a participant in The Big Year, a record-setting race of three birders in 1998 to identify the most bird species within the U.S.A. in one calendar year. Check out the book about the event – *The Big Year:*

A Tale of Man, Nature, and Fowl Obsession by Mark Obmascik. Who can resist a read with that title? An article in *The Plain Dealer* states that a movie is being made based on the book. I really hope that happens but who can predict the ways of moviemaking? Larry Rosche is also the author of *The Birds of the Cleveland Region.* (The movie *The Big Year*, shown in theaters 2011, was released on DVD January 2012. I've yet to see it but it is in my Netflix queue.)

I am an amateur birder, meaning I know enough to have fun, to identify some birds for less-informed friends, to participate in backyard feeder counting, but not enough to claim authority. I've been wrong too many times. My life list (a numbering of species seen in one's lifetime) stands at 193, but 88 of those were identified with the aid of a Kenyan guide while on an African safari. I've never taken a bird identification trip, nor do I take the time to rush off to local birding spots at the height of migrations or when an unusual sighting is broadcast. I do buy a bird book for each vacation site that's out of Ohio and attempt to find new birds on any trips. And I'm always watching for new birds that choose to fly through my backyard. This all qualifies me as an amateur bird watcher and I'm likely to stay that way.

Besides migrating birds, it is time again for the Lake MetroParks Canoe and Kayak Race. Postponed last weekend because the water was too high, it has been rescheduled for this Saturday. Canoes and kayaks loaded with racers will enter the Grand River in Ashtabula County at the Harpersfield Covered Bridge Metropark and paddle competitively (or not) downstream eight and a half miles to the Hidden Valley Metropark in Lake County at State Route 528 south of Madison.

Originally it was called the Mad Hatters Canoe Race and run by the Mad Hatters Canoe Club. I learn its history from Bob Bellas, an original member when the club was formed in 1966 (chartered 1968) and owner/operator of the Grand River Canoe Livery on Fobes Road in Ashtabula County. A group of local people met monthly for canoeing and camping. The first race was called the Hell Hollow Steeple Chase and run on Paine Creek, one of Grand River's tributaries in Lake County. All participants were encouraged to wear 'mad' hats.

Next the race was run from State Route 528 (Hidden Valley Metropark) all the way to Mason's Landing at Vrooman Road, but insufficient parking for the average 100 racers forced a move to the current location. It was named after either The Hatter in Lewis Carroll's *Alice's Adventures in Wonderland,* wherein Alice is warned by the Cheshire cat that the Hatter is mad, or after an Irish fairy tale – Mr. Bellas is not sure now what the source was. But the name stuck and by the end of their operation of the race, 300-400 people were participating even though the race was always scheduled for the third weekend in March when ice and snow were factors. Mr. Bellas does not recall the race ever being cancelled and was one of the planners who ran the river two weeks before each annual event to determine if there was too much ice. "But you could bet your life on a good snowstorm either the weekend before, or the race weekend, or the weekend after," he says. There were never any mishaps or accidents during the race, but he does recall prior to the race helping rescue a man and child who got caught in a hydraulic below the Harpersfield Dam and hearing of another man who drowned after becoming hypothermic, all of whom were practicing for the race. Participation in the Mad Hatters Canoe Club gradually waned and it was disbanded.

Since 1989, the race has been officiated by Lake Metroparks and is run at the end of April, thereby avoiding the issue of ice but not always snow. They have retained the maddest hat contest, the only rules being that the hat must be worn during the race and fit under the bridges. Each year the number of participants keeps increasing from the starting 227 in 1989. More and more people are running kayaks. Only about 30 racers wear contest hats. The rules also specify that prior experience is mandatory, but the interpretation of this policy is left up to the boater. There have been no accidents to date and only two postponements due to high water.

I won't see any racers at Blair Road Bridge since the race ends upstream at Hidden Valley Metropark, but it reminds me to do some planning for a spring kayak trip down the river. My daughter is having a gaggle of friends visit (mostly fellow RPCWs – Retired Peace Corps Workers) over Memorial Day weekend. Stereotypically, that's a group of people ready for adventure and maybe a day on the river.

52 GRAND RIVER CANOE LIVERY

July 2, 2009

The Grand River Canoe Livery, family owned and operated since 1966, is the oldest canoeing resource on the river and known for its quirkiness. You not only get canoe services but entertainment and education on both the river and American Indian ways, not to mention the spiritual airways all around. I arrive at the eastern section of Fobes Road in Ashtabula County because Bob Bellas, the owner, invited me after answering my questions over the phone about the defunct Mad Hatters Canoe Club.

This section of Fobes Road, a narrow, mostly gravel, two mile long road, ends at the best potholed driveway I've ever driven. I navigate my car slowly in and around the water-filled depressions and end at a lawn beside a two story, dark brown house. Bob greets me with an Indian phrase, the spelling of which is unknown, but phonetically sounds like "Ya-ta-hay." What he thought meant "hello," he was eventually told might mean "get the hell out of here." I don't and spend the next ninety minutes with him on a partially sunny, but mostly cloudy, warm summer afternoon.

Indian chants are being broadcast from the open garage door while Bob checks in a young couple renting a canoe. I wander around and check out what stuff is to be found under three uncanvassed tepee frames while he registers the man and woman at a picnic table under a huge black walnut tree. An Indian prayer on a rectangle of stretched canvas is in front of me. Another tepee across the driveway lists members of the Grand River Clan: Swims More than Paddles, Spandex Leghorn, Rolls out of Tipi, One Tough S.O.B., Sociable Rooster, Still Thinks He can Run, Limp Chicken, Hunter of Many Waters, River Dog and many others. Canoes are stacked in the back of the yard in front of a small barn, where an out-of commission blue van still has a readable advertisement: "Looking for something fun to do; call 1-800-ME-CANOE."

Out of the corner of my eye, I check out Bob who is dressed in a plaid shirt and blue jeans with a feather hanging from his headband. He carries a staff adorned with antlers, feathers, an animal skull and horn, leather thongs, and one strand of sleigh bells – the Magic Acorn Horn Stick. He regales his customers with stories and jokes while fulfilling his obligations for river safety. The young couple's faces look guarded, and they seem eager to move on to the river. I figure this is going to be an interesting interview. His eyes are gentle and his speech is measured. He knows what he's doing.

Bob started his livery in Painesville but moved here in 1972 ("or was it 1971?"). On workdays he drives to Painesville to manage his Ace Auto Top & Trim business. But these 40 acres in the middle of the Grand River Terraces is his obvious passion. His wife is a Cherokee Indian; he is of Polish descent. Only recently did they start to take an interest in her heritage for the sake of their seven children. "I look more Indian than any of them," Bob says. And he does, with his bronzed skin, lean body and brown eyes.

We walk on a mud and grass road past a Port-a-Potty, a barn, and a rack of lifejackets and oars. First he shows me Belly Acres, the ceremonial tepee with two memorial poles nearby extending thirty feet up into the blue skies. Every Memorial Day, veterans are honored by a pole-raising event. Guests tie Armed Services color-coded plastic ribbons to the pole, yell the veteran's name into the wind, and write his/her name on the stretched canvas. This is followed in the evening by the Sacred Circle bonfire beyond the tepee in a clearing downhill. Guests can claim an Indian name but they first must tell an acquisition story and then dance around the fire. The next day they feast.

Inside Belly Acres, light pours through the pole-crossed opening at the peak, highlighting a dirt floor and scattered items including a wild boar hide with a bullet hole and 14 stab marks. The story is that someone dumped seven Russian Saline pigs on Fobes Road about three years ago. As they grew, they started damaging the vegetation and worrying the residents. Bob, one of his sons, and a son-in-law participated in the round-up. The one they found ran away after it was shot. Tracking its blood trail, his son couldn't escape easily when the boar charged – hence the 14 knife stab scars on the hide.

I hear about the hawk that veered to flap his wings overhead while a woman was attaching a ribbon to the Ceremonial Pole. I learn about Cheerful Helping Brave, an eight-year-old orphaned boy afraid of the dark who was able to walk around the bonfire at his naming ceremony because two shadows came and accompanied him. I know there are many more stories inside Bob. He's a book by himself.

We walk on to the next tepee. This one is shorter and brown. Around it on the mowed paths and among the tall weeds are 23 staffs with ribbons for the 23 Brookpark Marines who all lost their lives within three days during the Iraq war. It's a surprisingly stirring memorial tucked in among the trees with the Grand River flowing somewhere nearby in the west. Inside the tepee are things that visitors have left: 'missing man's table', photos, POW-MIA flag, folded U.S.A. flag from a burial, buffalo skull, written prayers. I find I am holding my breath and release it slowly into the dedicated space. "It belongs to whoever wants to come; whatever they leave is fine," Bob says.

Continuing down the road, we enter more deeply into the woods, and soon reach a clearing with lots of upside down canoes. It's the Grand River at last, fifteen feet down, about twenty-five feet wide, full and brown, visibly flowing north. Looking over the steep bank, I think that launching a canoe here would be suicidal. Bob points out the hollowed dirt trail leading to a wood ramp fifteen feet beyond in the trees. That's better. I like how you have to walk to get to the launch site – the feeling of going deeper into nature and away from human habitation.

We move on to the next clearing where Bob-approved groups may camp. A father-and-son group has been coming for 22 years now to "deprogram the sons from their mothers' influences." The gathering now includes grandsons. Circling through more trees, we arrive back at the Sacred Circle. Bob mentions how the 2006 flood reached all the way up here- several hundred feet away and another ten feet up from the Grand River (Chapter 59).

I ask about available canoe trips. You can choose to stop at either of the two bridges ahead – Schweitzer Road (one hour) or Cold Springs Road (two hours) – or row on to Tote Road Township Park (3 ½ -4 hours), Mechanicsville Road (4 ½ -5 hours), or Harpersfield Dam (5 ½ -6 hours). He'll even rent the canoe for a two day trip if you want to go on past the dam. Bob is out on the river at least weekly in this upland region scouting for log jams, especially after storms. The water stays deep enough for canoeing all summer long, unlike the gorge section in Lake County where you can walk across the river in the hot months without getting your feet wet. It turns out that Bob was the U.S. Canoe Association's national champion in 1971 and 1972.

In addition to canoeing services, he offers a Native American ceremony and campfire at the Sacred Circle Dance site to groups like Scouts, Indian Guides and Princesses, Big Brothers, churches. And you can also spend a night in one of the other teepees tucked in among the trees.

He talks about the water monitoring and amphibian and animal species studies done nearby by organizations from the EPA to the Cleveland Museum of Natural History. He talks about how the Grand River is the cleanest water flowing into Lake Erie. I know he is just the kind of steward I want living along this river.

I assure him I will be back with some friends to canoe the river this weekend. He gives me wampum – not a string of shell beads – but a small wooden canoe complete with glued oars and his Grand River Canoe Livery slogan painted on its gunwale. I drive away slowly, savoring the peace and quiet and yet eager to invite my husband and friends to experience this place. I know they won't get the full treatment as I did nor feel as enchanted and refreshed by Bob, but the river will charm them, I'm sure. Oh, yes, the Magic Acorn Horn Stick predicts "with 100% accuracy 50% of the time" whether one will get wet when canoeing. If an acorn when shaken out of the horn lands on its bottom, it will be a dry run.

53 IT FEELS LIKE SPRING

Monday, May 9, 10:41 a.m., 62° F.

At least more warmth is here again – several days of sunny weather with temperatures in the seventies – all is well. The bird chorus in my backyard is rapturous. Lilac shrubs while only budded here are in full bloom in Painesville. I've switched from long pants to mid-calf ones for work. It's spring, it's spring!

At the Blair Road Bridge all seems quiet except for birdsong and the river's music. Two rapids are now visible, and their gentle splashing is barely heard above the river's hum. Gravel beds along the banks and in the channel are visibly dried. The water is now a semi-translucent black tea color. Deciduous trees are half-leafed. It's spring, it's spring!

I see bank swallows swooping and diving for insects over the river. The high south bluff is just what the smallest member of the North American swallow family prefers for its burrows. It uses its bill to make a hole and then its feet to fashion a tunnel, up to five to six feet long. Both sexes dig and nest and feed the young – three to seven offspring are common. And they do it twice each year. No wonder there is so much fluttering and swooping over the river for insects. I would love to see their courtship ritual of dropping and catching feathers in flight. Even though there are lots of the swallows, birdsong doesn't seem as loud here as at home. Different habitat? Trees and shrubs are close by my house while here at the Grand River there are more open spaces with some grasslands along the banks and older trees inland. I look for the Canada goose I saw last week, but it's not here.

A lone fisherman stands in front of my log seat, his line trolling the river. The water there on the outside of a gentle big curve averages three feet deep. Three trucks are parked farther up the road, but I see only the one fisherman.

Yesterday was a perfect spring day too. It was great weather for the Canoe and Kayak Race sponsored by Lake Metroparks. I'm glad the race stops at State Route 528. I like thinking that rarely do canoes and kayaks run the stretch from Hidden Valley Park past the Blair Road Bridge to Mason's Landing at Vrooman Road. That's the problem with great locations. Once discovered you want them all for yourself and yet can't help telling others. On the flip side, if more people see this lovely river valley, maybe more will support its preservation.

As I snap my photos at least six vehicles pass by. One slows as I am opening my car door. The driver calls, "Are you all right?" It surprises me that every person who has inquired about me on the bridge has assumed there might be a problem. I appreciate the concern, but given the setting why doesn't he/she think I am viewing the scenery? Perhaps I shouldn't leave my car's emergency lights on. "Oh, hi, Margie," he adds. It's Tom who lives two miles from my house. "I'm taking pictures," I reply. He continues up the hill. I want to add, "I'm writing a book about the Grand River." It feels important and thrilling to me, this chronicle of my visits to the river. Will it interest anyone else?

At the top of the north hill I search the properties for a donkey. I see one black horse. Okay, it might have been a harsh neighing that I heard last week. I'd prefer to have found a donkey. Farther down the road, there are white domestic ducks at a small pond. I'm glad not all houses in this area look like suburbia with manicured lawns and only a cat or dog. Give me a goat, a donkey, a goose, a chicken, a swan instead. But not too near the Grand River. I wouldn't want fertilizers and manure to pollute the pristine water of this mighty river that flows through my county.

54 SPRING RITUALS

Monday, May 16, 4:50 p.m., 62° F.

The sporadic warm-up continues. After several days of rain and unseasonably low temperatures, the sun is no longer shrouded by clouds. Its rays play on the Grand River on both sides of the bridge. Bank swallows sail and swoop over the western water. The air is soft and light. Most of the trees are fully leafed, but my favorite sycamore on the northeast flood zone is still only budded; at least it's not dead as I feared. Plant life underneath the trees is flourishing. The Grand River's flood zones are dominated by ostrich fern, skunk cabbage, and false hellebore – an unusual grouping for Ohio. Just another thing that makes this rippled ribbon of charcoal-colored water special.

Several cars are parked off the road halfway up the north hill, but I don't see any fishermen in the river – maybe they are around the upstream bend. In between hearing vehicles carrying neighbors home from work, I listen to the sounds of the full river. On the eastern bend, I hear and then see a small rapid, but a louder gurgling nearby draws my attention. Peering over the east bridge railing, I see a six-inch tree trunk anchored between the riverbed's rocks and the wire-wrapped stone embankment – just enough disturbance in the water to make music. I wonder when this small trunk will get swept away.

My log seat has been rearranged by the many high waters this spring. I would love to go and sit again for an hour, but there's no time today. Even though I have only three more trips planned to the Blair Road Bridge to complete this year-long project, I've still got things I want to do – another hour-long sit, another canoe trip, driving over all the river's bridges (Appendix C). Will there be enough time yet this year?

Spring rituals are getting in the way. We have a party planned for Memorial Day weekend. All my garden beds need weeding and mulching. I want to buy plants for old buckets that I collect. Weeds are crowding out the mosses on the brick walkway. The picnic tables and benches have to be removed from the porch of the Slanty Shanty and arranged around the fire pit – that's a two-person job. And then there is the menu planning, grocery shopping, and housecleaning. Did I mention we are leaving July 1st for Maho Bay Camps on St. Johns Island in the U.S. Virgin Islands? In exchange for working six hours (making beds, fixing broken sewer lines, stocking the small store, etc.) five days each week for one month, we get free room and board at this eco-friendly tent compound built among the trees on hills surrounding a lovely bay. Sounds heavenly.

I have mixed feelings about the end of this project, sometimes almost a paralyzing malaise. What is that all about? I am still seeing the Grand River but feel my attention waning. I do have at least a year's research ahead of me, but I welcome that. I can't believe how fast this year has come and gone, but it is nothing compared to the river's existence. Maybe that's it. I'm mortal; the river is not.

I think again of the American Indians who first canoed the river. Has little changed along its banks for most of its length? Would they recognize its bends, gravel beds, and rapids? I wish the names they had for its topography were still known. And if I could come back in one hundred years, would I recognize my year's study spot?

55 THEY MADE IT

Tuesday, May 24, 4:15 p.m., 62° F.

This is a blustery spring day with echoes of winter. The temperature is the same as when I last visited eight days ago, but it feels colder. The trees are all fully leafed except for the sycamores. Sunlight reflected on the water highlights the wind-created ripples that appear to go upstream. High overhead, big blue/gray cumulus clouds scurry toward the east. When they block the sun's rays, the temperature drops a few degrees. When the gusty northeast wind hits me, I pull the collar of my fleece jacket higher and hug myself.

Along the base of the southwest bluff, several large pieces of broken rock dot the curved slope at the water's edge. They look like stepping stones only mountain goats could navigate. Eastern hemlock saplings grow randomly above horizontal shale lines halfway up the bluff, their darker green needles distinct against the new green of the deciduous trees. Some shrubs attempt to maintain their purchase on the lower half of the bluff near freshet sites, but like those stones, they may tumble to the water someday.

East of the bridge, I see two Canada geese with one gosling. I can't believe it. These two geese managed to make a nest somewhere around here and hatch an offspring. After I noticed that the gravel bed they were frequenting was submerged under water with the last rain, I assumed their nest was destroyed. Maybe some eggs were lost since there is only one gosling. Do the adult geese learn from this experience or will they be back next spring to the same locale?

At my house I'm enjoying the return of a ruby-throated hummingbird. I wait each year until I see one before putting up the glass globe feeder with its port holed red plastic bottom. This year I am buzzed. While kneeling in the front of the house pulling weeds out of a flowerbed, a hummingbird appeared and circled my head before flying to the nearby serviceberry shrub. Say what you will, I think the hummingbird was announcing its arrival and urging me to put up its feeder. I've read somewhere that the same hummingbirds come back to the same feeding sites – all the way from Mexico. I went inside, washed and filled the feeder, then hung it on a back porch hook. A male hummingbird showed up within ten minutes to drink my concocted nectar. The female usually arrives later but stays longer in the fall. Eventually there will be three or four of them fighting over one globe, although there are three globes side-by-side. From now on I am going to record arrival and departure dates of these flying marvels.

The spring peepers, northern leopard frogs, green frogs and

bullfrogs are out of hibernation too. The seasonal home entertainment has begun. The Grand River is well into spring too, but its water temperature will rise slowly as long as spring rain keeps adding to its volume.

Oh my, news flash. In looking over my past writings, I discover that I need only two more visits to the Blair Road Bridge to complete 52 observations. My Microsoft numbering is amiss, and somehow two of the essays were not entered in the computer. Hurray for a paper trail. The end of this project is coming sooner that I thought.

56 ONE MORE CANOE RIDE

July 5, 2009

This time I select the upland section where the river has a muddy bottom. Colby, Jan and Debe, plus friends Carl and Joanne drive in two cars over country roads east across Ashtabula County to end up on the potholed driveway of the Grand River Canoe Livery. I watch them as they are greeted by Bob Bellas and observe the Native American atmosphere. Joanne does the Magic Acorn Horn Stick toss, which predicts a dry run for us. After visits to the Port-A-Potty, we walk the dirt roadway that leads to the riverbank.

Along the way I show them the Ceremonial Tipi (Bob's spelling choice) with its memorial poles and the Memorial Tipi with its honor staffs. At the river, we select our canoes and slide them down the ramp into the twenty-five foot wide Grand River. Its brown color is rich and impenetrable; its steady current pushes our canoes along at a slow pace. The air is warm with temperatures in the 70s, and sunlight appears around the billowing clouds overhead. Mature trees and shrubs line the banks and overhang the water. Birdsong is all around. It's a perfect day to canoe.

Each couple attempts to set ground rules for paddling. Colby says I should do what I want when I want, and he'll compensate from the rear seat. Someone requests we all stop talking. When we do, we are rewarded by an undisturbed full river pulling us downstream. There are no homes in this section, which is part of the Grand River Terraces. The predominant tree is some type of willow with huge trunks and large branches ending in small, pointy leaves. We mostly glide as the current carries us but need steerage to negotiate around and over fallen trunks and limbs coming from the banks, sometimes seemingly straddling the river. There is always a way to get through or around the debris. No one tips or stalls for long. The muddy banks with blackened soil and flattened grasses show that the water level was higher recently.

Although the river bends and turns, the curves are mild. We are heading north. There were other people getting ready to enter the river when we departed, but we do not see nor hear them behind us. It's so great to be alone on this wild and scenic river. After about forty minutes we come to the metal truss bridge at Schweitzer Road and see and hear a few vehicles pass overhead. A corral of ten canoes is awaiting a van – their time on the river over. Our greetings are pleasantly minimal as we float by – mostly comments on the perfect day.

My attention returns to the cold water on my fingertips as I trail my hand in the dark brown, soil-laden river. Our paddles do not touch bottom. This river is like a half-tube through flatlands on both sides above the ten foot high banks. We pass one empty shack with a ragged, screened-in porch. A flock of red-winged blackbirds and one scarlet tanager decorate tree branches. We go by within three feet of two sunning turtles. We debate if the narrow swaths of smoothed mud on the banks are otter slides. A hawk takes flight.

Soda cans are popped open and apples crunched. We come together, go apart, and switch leads – sometimes the only evidence of our passage the clunk of an oar on the canoe's gunwale or the splashing of water from a turned paddle. At one point a chain saw disturbs the nature sounds but, mercifully, it doesn't sound long. We pass a clot of canoes with beer-drinkers stalled in the river, but even they are not raucous and, from their comments, also appreciate the river and weather today. Farther on we see a fisherman maneuvering his canoe back upstream by pulling on low hanging branches. The river continues in a secluded channel with no visible buildings. We spot a large, leatherback turtle on the east bank. Was its shell three feet long? No, Carl, the rest of us think it wasn't over two feet in length.

Just before the next bridge on Cold Springs Road, we see the first property with land cleared down to the river. The white farmhouse and red barn are surrounded by lawn down to the west bank. There's no evidence of farmed fields or livestock. The river is broader now, at least seventy-five feet wide. Another house of A-frame construction is nestled among the trees on the east side. The metal of the long, modern cement bridge reflects the shimmering water as we pass under its span. Bob had said that after this bridge we would start to see houses – yes, but few and far between still. Most are partially hidden by trees and vegetation, but every now and then some homeowner has cleared the land to the river's edge. How unattractive that is, and potentially detrimental for the river. It's usually a new home – those people need some education about riparian setbacks.

We paddle on looking for a brown house with a surrounding wood deck. It's the clue that predicts only another twenty minutes left to paddle before the takeout ramp at Tote Road Township Park. But I think we have at least another hour to go. In my mind's eye I review the river's route as outlined on an Ohio map. There's a bend to the west before the takeout spot, and we are still canoeing north. Along this stretch some homes (primarily on the east bank) have erected artificial banks, and some have tethered pontoon boats. I feel proud of our quiet journey. Rarely, we see people out on decks or moored boats. We note one man sitting still and silent in a lawn chair facing the river on a high bank. He does not acknowledge our passage – maybe he is so lost in reverie that he didn't see us. Whatever, it surely seems an inviting way to spend the afternoon.

We keep seeing brown houses with decks, but then the obviously intended one appears with a three-sided deck. Now it should be twenty minutes to the takeout, but the river is still heading north – no turn west yet. We need to paddle more often now in the slower current and wider, fuller river. The waterscape still feels secluded with mostly trees and fields to the west and nestled homes in the east. At last, the river bends ninety degrees west, and the late afternoon sun, aligned with the river, shines directly on our faces.

Oh, look, another brown house with a surrounding deck. Is this the marker and there is still another twenty minutes to go? No, the next house has a pale green roof as also predicted, and directly across the river is the cement ramp at the park. We have arrived. I'm not particularly tired from our three hours and forty minutes canoeing, but I am relieved to stand and stretch my body. Within ten minutes Bob shows up with his van and canoe trailer. Singlehandedly, he lifts the canoes above his head and walks each one up the incline to his trailer's racks. Somehow in the course of packing our gear into the van, Carl is given the Indian name of Ten Foot Alligator.

We rave about our trip and Grand River's beauty on the ride back to the livery. Bob gives each couple some wampum – a four-inch round curio with its scene of mountains, snow, river, eagle and Indian plus 1-800-ME-CANOE inked on its edge. Too bad he doesn't have a picture of our river. And now we get to drive back to our house over rural roads. It's been a memorable day and an entirely different canoeing experience than that of the river's run in Lake County. The Grand River continually shows its depth and might here, never running thin. I want to come back.

57 NINE FISH

Thursday, June 2, 4:45 p.m., 78° F.

The water has cleared – I can see at least three feet down. On the east side of the bridge, large yellow slabs of stone are visible under the water halfway across the river. Just beyond them, the water turns deep blue/black, obscuring the bottom. West of the bridge I see more protruding slabs with deeper waters on the inside of the river's bend. Something is moving in the translucent water – nine fish at least a foot or more in length are headed upstream – one dark maroon/brown, the others olive green/yellow. Slowly advancing upstream, they wiggle their tails and fins for a few seconds and then seem to rest without sliding backwards before moving ahead again. I lose sight of them when they enter the shadows under the bridge.

The weather is so pleasant – warm, sunny, balmy with only the slightest breeze. I decide to walk the length of the bridge both ways. Vehicles are passing every few minutes, so I hug the guardrail and stand still when they pass until I realize when one car comes too close for comfort that it might be better to be moving. It's unusual to see so many cars on the bridge, but it is late afternoon when daytime workers are going home. There are enough breaks between cars that I can gaze into the water below but I don't see any fish. Are they stalled under the bridge or did they seek deeper water where I can't see them? Is this a journey for spawning? It seems late for that. They may not make it back out of here because soon the water level will be low and stay so through summer.

The sycamore tree is still not completely leafed. I have been checking out other sycamore trees on my way to and from work. None of them are completely leafed either. Their mottled white trunks with meager buds and leaves make them look like snags from a distance. At least now I know for sure that my favorite sycamore is not dying – just taking its time. I look up sycamore diseases and find that the trees are susceptible to Plane anthracnose fungus. The fungus appears after the leaves have expanded causing them to brown, shrivel, and fall. In early July the trees put forth a second crop of leaves, effectively shortening its growing season. It doesn't sound like a problem with my sycamore but I'll keep watching.

No fishermen are at the river today. They don't know what they are missing. I scan for the Canada goose and its gosling, but cannot find them. Other birds are chattering overhead, and an occasional bank swallow scoops the air above the water for insects. Just another grand day at the Grand River.

With only one more official visit to go on this project, I think about what it has meant to me. Viewing the same site and sight carefully on a weekly basis has made the river more present. My recollections add an emotional weight that wasn't there before. I claim the river's existence in my thoughts as my reward for putting forth the effort to study its course. I am thankful for the images of the seasons upon the water. I shall probably become a nuisance. I am so bursting with the nuances of this experience that I may be compelled to offer some tidbit whenever the Grand River comes up in conversations. And even if I get corrected or disbelieved or avoided, I will feel content and maybe a little superior because I carry with me the memories of my time along an American river.

58 THE LAST SIT

Tuesday, June 7, 2 p.m., 85° F.

Getting out of my parked car at the Grand River, I hear the bell tower announce the hour with its song followed by two chimes. I have my trekking pole, binoculars, camera, and drink. I have sufficiently screened and sprayed my skin for sun and bugs. I plan to spend an hour by the river on this last project visit. I negotiate the sharp bank at the top of the path gingerly – there's no pain, only my hesitation – my new left knee works. Purple phlox and yellow marsh irises light my way between the high grasses to the open banks. The water, looking like weak tea, is only one to three feet deep and flows along slowly, barely six inches above the rocks of the small rapid directly ahead. Just the right combination for a gentle gurgling.

It's a hot, humid day – more of a summer day than a spring one. Heading east, I pick my way along the spongy, muddy, debris-strewn bank toward my sitting spot on the large fallen tree before the next bend in the river. Across the water, I see two forest green plastic lawn chairs positioned behind some grasses on a gravel bed. They are probably the property of one of the two homes' residents. I understand the impulse and can imagine myself sitting there in the morning or early evening but would prefer not to see the chairs on this visit.

I continue along the river to the fallen trunk and find the bleached forked limb that just fit my body before. This time I can't seem to get comfortable; I keep sliding to my right. I suspect the higher spring waters rolled it somewhat. I pull out my drink and a celebratory chocolate bar, which I must eat right away because it is melting.

A bar of chocolate, a turquoise dragonfly resting on a branch near my elbow, a bank swallow over the water, a yellow butterfly downstream, and far-off, the plaintive sounds of a mourning dove all next to a sun-dappled river – could it be any better? I think not. Mostly the breeze is light – enough to cool the sweat collecting at my neck, but occasionally its strength coming through the cottonwoods makes enough sound to rival the splashing of two small rapids – one on my right and one on my left.

I hear the bell tower sound the quarter hour. The sun has moved enough that now I am in full light and I feel too far from the river. I move to sit on its bank, my feet dangling an inch above the water and my body in the full shade created by a live tree's far-reaching branch. The soil is soft and its moisture dampens my pants. That feels good too.

The water flows by carrying a load of white fluffy cottonwood tufts. Others gently float up, down, and by on the air. The log on the other side of the river is definitely farther up on the gravel bank than before – no water reaches it. From my new vantage point, the green plastic lawn chairs are now hidden by a tall patch of grass. Looking at the Class I rapids that extend all the way across the river, I doubt that a kayak could navigate past without scraping or stalling on rocks.

Sensing movement on my left, my eyes are drawn to a great blue heron stalking the shallows on the south bank. I get out my binoculars and watch off and on. When the bird is standing still, one would think it was a branch.

Within five minutes of each other, two small aircraft lumber overhead, their engine noises disturbing my reverie, their shadows large on the land. The great blue heron is walking slowly my way along the river's edge. Then I lose sight of it and cannot find it again, although I look every few minutes or so with my binoculars. I suspect it has ventured into the tall grasses.

The bell tower sounds every fifteen minutes. I start shooting some photos, reserving three exposures for my usual three shots when I leave. Nothing much and yet everything happens along the Grand River. The hour passes; the bell tolls three times. The great blue heron appears about one hundred feet up in the sky following the curve of the river. It flies by me and on over the bridge, heading west, the river sounds masking the music its wings must make as they undulate up and down. A woodpecker's repetitive tapping overrides all the other bird songs.

I rise to stand in the water near the rapids. The lukewarm water fills my shoes and cools my ankles. Fifteen minutes after three o'clock I make my way back up the path and walk along the side of the road back to my car in shoes swishing in Grand River water.

59 A FLOOD IN MY TIME

July 27 and July 28, 2006

It has been thirteen months since my last deliberate visit to the Blair Road Bridge to collect impressions and take photos of the Grand River for my book. And on this first anniversary Lake County has coincidentally experienced a 100-year flood. My Grand River has shown what she is capable of when the sky dumps mucho rain on Lake County. I could not believe such a momentous event occurred before I was finished with this book.

This summer has already been one of the wettest on record. One week ago there was another heavy rainstorm in the late afternoon and by bedtime water was rolling across our backyard and filling the driveway depression in front of the garage. Colby, who was away on a business trip, could only appreciate the event by my excited description over the phone.

I called my father to report that his worries about my house being flooded were unfounded. When the overflow from Rana Pond is too much for my backyard swale, the water just cruises across the rest of the lawn and not into my house. The northern pond edge must be just high enough to direct the water farther west where the land slopes ever so slightly northward. Both Dad and I were relieved.

So you have the scenario – a summer of unusual rain, the ground saturated, my Rana Pond full – any more rain has nowhere to go but as run-off. It rains sporadically all day Thursday, July 27. At bedtime, around 9:30 p.m., there's an inch of rain in the rainfall gauge. While Colby and I are reading in bed I notice the rainfall is getting heavier and harder. I decide to stop reading and enjoy the rain drumming on our asphalt roof and twanging on the tin covering over the front porch just outside the open bedroom window. Its rhythm lulls me to sleep, but I'm having a hard time staying asleep. The rain wakes me up now and again as it crescendos and decrescendos.

Around midnight I decide to look out the windows because, if the pond is overflowing again, I want my husband to see it. Wow, is it ever! The entire backyard from the rear deck to the edge of the wood is a river of water heading north. "Colby, wake up. You've got to see this. It's worse than last week." I point out that the five inch rain gauge is full. I venture outside to empty it, getting completely soaked in the process.

Downstairs we find a flashlight to look more closely at the stream of three to four inches of water flowing over the backyard. At the front of the house, the driveway depression beyond the garage doors' ramp has four inches of rain pooled over the four-inch drainpipe grate.

The water also overlaps the front brick walkway, creeping toward our porch, which is only one step up and level with the front door.

"Wow, can you believe it? This is something." Back upstairs we go. "Look at that! There's another half inch of water in the rain gauge already."

I sleep fitfully (always wanted to say that), but hours go by in which I am unaware of the rainstorm. The alarm clock shrills at 6:45 a.m. I rush to the rain gauge – another four inches! "We've had nine inches of rain overnight! I'm going outside to look around."

The rain has stopped, but the overflowing continues in the backyard. I need my knee-high boots to wade through the driveway pool. I reach down to find the drain – it's clear – the water is just coming too fast for the pipe to handle. I continue on to the end of my driveway. The culvert is overflowing, and water runs over the end of our driveway; half of its gravel washed away to a depth of four inches. What is that louder roar? Can the small unnamed stream in the road dip be making that clamor?

I walk 150 feet to the culvert and stare at the brown rushing 'river' now racing under the road. My neighbor, George, whose property includes the stream and the remains of an old bridge over the unused road that used to head west into Hell Hollow, is out looking too. "I came out at 4 a.m., and the water was going over the road," he says. I note the pressed vegetation. "It took out the two beams of the old bridge. There's nothing left now," he says. I wonder where the beams will be found because I have walked this creek, and it quickly disappears into thick vegetation that narrows the creek bed to less than two feet wide. It's at least another 500 feet before the creek gains more width. However, this morning all bets are off, and this creek has new life and power.

George relates that Thompson Road has lost some of its pavement and may be impassable going east. How will I get to work, I wonder. Every road out of here has creeks to cross. Reluctantly I head back to my house, but I get ready for work fast because I want to see the Grand River at Blair Road Bridge before I attempt to get out of the township and head for Ashtabula.

Driving north on Brockway Road, I admire all the full ditches. On Trask Road, I see a pick-up truck approaching and flag it down. It's Doug, the son of another neighbor a few houses north of ours. "If you're going south, I heard that LeRoy Road is closed." I tell him.

"No, I'm just going to my uncle's right here, but let me show you something," he replies. And on his cell phone I see the missing road section on Thompson Road, and the SUV trapped by a fallen tree on top of a landslide on Blair Road beyond the bridge. "You can't go east on

Trask or Balch either; I don't know about Ford."

Off I rush to the Grand River. I'm not the only one. There's a car stopped at the south end of the bridge, and the Slender Man from the Tudor house is walking on the bridge. The water is within six inches of the bottom of the bridge – huge and brown and roaring and spectacular. The flood zones north on both sides of the road are flooded as far as I can see into the trees. I walk across the bridge to catch a glimpse of the swamped SUV and mudslide halfway up the north hill. The road is completely blocked.

"Have you ever seen the river this high?" I ask after learning the man in the car lives somewhere just up the hill. Both men say probably not, although sometimes in winter when the ice starts to break up and chokes the river, there's as much overflow into the flood zones. They estimate that the water is thirteen feet higher than its springtime depth.

A monster additional thirteen feet of water all heading downstream toward the Vrooman Road Bridge and Mason's Landing Metropark before snaking into Painesville and the bridges on Walnut Street (SR 84) and Main Street! I think about the fact that the lower land around the Main Street bridge is crowded with condominiums, some older houses and a car repair shop on the east side. This area was inundated in both the 1893 and 1913 floods. Farther downstream is the Richmond Street Bridge, which marks the beginning of a multitude of docked boats from there to Lake Erie. I wonder what happened there last night when the river peaked.

But I have to go to work. Ford Road is passable although at the deep ravine of Talcott Creek, a third of the road is missing. I wonder how Shannon and her family did overnight. (I met her when she served on the Board for my employer). Their house sits next to Talcott Creek, tucked between the streambed and steep hills. Do they have flood insurance because I realize there is no way they didn't have flooding last night? I can only catch a glimpse of the house back through the trees. The water is back in the creek's channel.

All day at work in Ashtabula, the radio gave details of the Flood of the Century (as they first dubbed it). Later the reporters decided it was ONLY a 500 year flood – meaning such a flood only happens once every 500 years. Between noon on Thursday and 9 a.m. on Friday, up to 9.7 inches of rain fell on Lake County – more than a half-gallon for every square foot of land according to *The Plain Dealer,* but my engineer husband calculates it was six gallons per square foot and gives me the formula to prove it.

The Grand River reached a new high at Fairport Harbor – 17.36 feet at 5:30 a.m., more than four feet over the prior record of 13.1 feet.

One man was drowned trying to remove a dump truck from a flooded Eastlake marina. His body was found on Saturday in the Mentor Lagoons. From 3 a.m. until morning's light, some residents were pulled from their second story windows at the Gristmill and Millstone Condominiums near the Main Street Bridge in Painesville. Boats still attached to portions of docks and the floating carnival bar from Pickle Bill's Restaurant in the village of Grand River were washed into Lake Erie and videotaped from helicopters flying over the disaster. No one else was missing or hurt, but hundreds were displaced, their homes or condominiums ruined. Northeast Ohio made the national TV news. The governor declared a state of emergency in Lake County and on August 1st the area was given a Federal Disaster designation.

We were safe and dry and spent the evening glued to the TV after driving down to see the huge hole in Thompson Road. The culvert there is big enough for a car to drive through, but the water's volume and force was so great that the entire road was washed away – the gouge as big as the culvert still intact right next to the mammoth hole. Colby climbed down to its bottom and you could have piled at least four men on top of each other's shoulders and barely reached the roadbed where I stood. It'll be awhile before this section is repaired.

Later, I learn that in Lake County two bridges and two culverts on tributaries of the Grand River were washed away. All the bridges on the river remain intact although debris piled up at several of them, especially at Vrooman Road. According to the U.S. Geological Survey, at the peak of the flood about 224,200 gallons per second of water rushed down the Grand River – about triple the average flow and fifteen feet higher than normal. The river was back in its channel within twenty-four hours. The cleanup and repairs are going to take a lot longer and the flooding is now due to "a 1000 year, 48 hour rain."

Now I know what the Grand River can do when you give it a lot of water. Now I can visualize how it has shaped the land, formed the valleys and flood plains, and carved the bluffs. It deserves its name. It certainly has earned even more of my respect.

March 17, 2009

It's easy to understand why Shannon and her husband, Tim, bought the fourteen acres along Talcott Creek fifteen years ago. There's a steep hill both east and west on Ford Road before I enter their driveway next to the creek in the ravine. Over 300 feet in the distance sits a two story house with a screened, triangular porch on the creek side. The water murmurs and gurgles constantly as the creek winds from the south around the house on its east side, next to a clump of eastern hemlocks on the forested bluff before dropping over a five foot waterfall and through the culvert under Ford Road. The Grand River waits about a mile farther north to accept the creek's water.

Flood insurance was not required when Shannon and Tim built the house. The 100 feet of land between the bluffs was not a flood plain, only a 100 year flood zone. In eight years since the house was built, Talcott Creek was never over its banks, only going up and down with rainfalls. But that all changed on Thursday night, July 27, 2006.

When Shannon returned from her book club meeting at 11 p.m., the creek was running full from all the recent rain but not over its banks. The sump pump in the basement was running, its rumble annoying to Shannon and Tim in their first floor bedroom at the front of the house, so Shannon went upstairs to lie with Delaney, age three, and Marcus, age five. At midnight, Tim hollered up the stairs, "It sounds like a waterfall. Get out of the house now!" It was so noisy Tim was afraid the house was going to come apart. He took a few seconds to grab some papers out of a floor safe and place them up higher in the bedroom. Shannon threw some clothes on the kids and herself before coming down the stairs and stepping in six inches of water on the first floor. Tim grabbed Marcus while calling Shannon's father on his cell phone, "Come pick us up; we need a ride."

Each with a child in their arms, Tim and Shannon opened the northwest door and got swept away by the raging creek when they stepped out onto their stoop. The current carried them around the west side of the house into the first stand of trees just beyond their attached garage and a parking area. Tim and Marcus were able to grab on, but Shannon, with Delaney hanging around her neck, was carried on down the driveway in the debris-loaded waters. Delaney was crying, and Shannon was screaming for Tim. They were stopped by a two-trunked tree. Shannon braced her back against one trunk and hugged the other one with her legs. The water came up to their waists.

At first Shannon and Tim could hear each other, but soon the

149

rain and roar of the water in the 200 feet between them interfered. Somehow Tim and Marcus, who were only twenty-five feet from the western bluff, were able to scramble through the trees with its understory of blackberry vines and make their way to the top of the bank. His cell phone had gotten wet and wouldn't work. No one was home at the house perched at the ravine's edge. He walked south to another house but no one answered his knocking. Reversing his steps north along the ravine he found help across the road at the fourth house he tried. The farmer later used his tractor to secure a rope to the rescue boat.

Shannon, in her nightgown, raincoat, socks, and Teva sandals, was holding Delaney, clothed only in a nightgown over underpants and socks. As the water continued to rise, she climbed the tree without losing her bracing between the two trunks. While initially afraid she was going to die, Shannon thought to herself, "This is not how it's going to end. I won't be that dead person in a tree in a flood." She couldn't see in the pitch black night and didn't know how close to the Ford Road culvert they were. Figuring that being swept into or through the culvert would be the end, she found holds on small branches on the two trunks and inched herself upward. "Ok, Delaney, raise your arms and grab a branch. Count one, two, three, then pull." That way, she kept her body halfway out of the water. Delaney, who sat facing her mother, stopped crying once they were in the tree.

Shannon thought it was important to keep her talking and/or singing but eventually in the four hours they spent there, Delaney said, "Mommy, I don't have anything else to talk about," and fell asleep. For the first two hours the water kept rising; then the rain stopped and as the water receded slowly, Shannon and Delaney retreated somewhat down the tree. Shannon wondered if this was the tree where the family's canoe was tethered at its base. Wouldn't that be ironic, she thought. But the canoe, which survived the onslaught too, was halfway between her savior tree and the house. She took off Delaney's socks because it seemed strange to her to have them on without any shoes. One she threw away in the dark, the other one she hung on a branch at their heads thinking it would be good for a laugh later if they found out they had only been about three feet above the ground. She was grateful her eyeglasses hadn't been torn off her face. "I don't know about you, but I can't be without my contact lenses or glasses," she said.

The first time the fire trucks arrived from the east, she could see their lights on the hill. The water was over the culvert and road, filling the bottom of the ravine. The truck could not get through to the other side where the driveway was and left to go around on the next road north. But they couldn't get across the Blair Road Bridge either to come in from the west because a mudslide has blocked the north hill. It would be two more hours before they were able to get to her from the east side. She had to watch their headlights recede up the hill, aware her screaming wasn't being heard.

Shannon's father somehow drove in next from the east after the rain had stopped. Shannon had lost track of time. By then he could drive over the culvert and up the west hill to walk along the bluff with a flashlight while yelling, "Shannon, Shannon!" He found her and Delaney when his flashlight reflected off her eyeglasses and then they could hear each other's yells. He said that Tim and Marcus were okay although Shannon wondered if he was just telling her that to reassure her while she was trapped in the ravine.

Two of the firefighters who finally floated to them in a boat tethered to the farmer's tractor were parents of students in Shannon's high school classes. "Shannon, what are you doing in this tree?" one of them said. At 4:30 a.m. they were out of the water. At 5:30 a.m, they made it to Tim's parents' house in north Madison. No one was hurt. Shannon was amazed by the leaves and sticks all over Delaney and herself when they got into the bathtub. Tim later got a tetanus shot because of all the scratches from the blackberry bushes. And two days later, every muscle in Shannon's body was sore. They had survived the 2006 flood.

Twelve hours later, Tim and Shannon returned to Talcott Creek, but not before first calling a neighbor to go look at their house and prepare them for what they were going to see. "We don't think you're going to live there again, honey," was the reply. When they arrived there was no water in their yard, house, or basement. The creek flowed again completely within its channel. The screened porch was intact, but the home's foundation was all in the basement. Only metal posts were supporting the house. It was all those concrete chunks banging around in the basement that had made Tim think the house was coming down. All the windows on the first floor were okay, but everything in the living room had been pushed up against the kitchen counters. The ninety-year-old neighbor who lived just above the west bluff had "never seen anything like it." (He was born after the 1913 flood.)

One year later almost to the very day of the flood, Tim, Shannon, Marcus, and Delaney moved back into the house, which had been redesigned; its reinforced foundation now had flood vents in the walls. Soil was brought in to extend the land south of the house – now the creek bed is farther away and curves sooner to the east before running north. "We didn't want to start all over. FEMA helped with the cleanup and rebuilding by providing a second mortgage at a low interest rate,"

Shannon says. So did lots of neighbors, relatives, friends, and even strangers. Everything that could be salvaged was, even the utility room sink with its paint stains from the first time the house was decorated. Each recovered CD was washed one at a time. The house was gutted to its studs on both floors. Since mold had appeared upstairs, new insulation and drywall was installed before all the rooms were painted in their original colors. The bottom kitchen cabinets had to be replaced, but the top ones only needed cleaning. The first floor half bath needed a new sink and Shannon got an old pedestal one from her father's barn that she had always coveted.

The children did not see the property again for three or four months until all the debris had been removed. Then they spent a lot of time playing in the creek and having fun outdoors, remembering why they liked the place so much. They sleep well at night now, even during rainstorms; they believe their parents will keep them safe. Marcus doesn't like to talk about the flood but wandered onto the porch during my interview. As Shannon is showing me the only high water mark left in the house (on the patio door), Marcus backs up to the door. "I'm four feet, two inches tall," he says. His curly blond hair was two inches below the horizontal water stain. Delaney will talk about it, and just that week for a classroom assignment had written on a paper, "I am brave becus I clibed a tree dering the flood."

Tim doesn't like to talk about it either but installed a high water alarm in the ground near the creek. There have been four nights so far that they have chosen not to spend in the house. The choice to move back wasn't easy, but Shannon "loves it so much." And I agree. It's an idyllic setting although she's not sure how many more years she will want to snowblow the long driveway. Over 125 people attend the flood anniversary parties. Their home insurance company helped them get flood insurance. And Delaney looks at her sock everyday, still eighteen feet up in the rescue tree secured by a nail and marked by a yellow plastic tie around the trunk.

AFTERWORD

Several changes have occurred at the Blair Road Bridge. Perry Township has erected a sign just beyond the bridge heading north that marks the beginning of their territory. I liked it better without the sign. One trunk of my favorite sycamore tree fell and now lies stretched on the land toward the river. With only two of its three trunks left, the tree is weakened, and the hollow at its base is further exposed to weather.

The road department has reworked the northeast embankment twice, extending the wall of chiseled stones along the river. The last effort seems to have stopped the erosion there, but now the path down to the river is gone, and the hillside is too steep for me to navigate standing up. That would require completely trusting my metal left knee and ignoring the pain I now have in my right knee.

For a while at the top of the north hill, there was a sign by the side of the road declaring: "Cabras para vente" – goats for sale. My goats for sale? That sign is now gone, and so are the goats - the pasture is empty.

Finally, there are large, black arrows on gold rectangle signs down both hills to the river. Were not the guiderails with their nighttime reflectors adequate for safe driving? I hate the signs and how they intrude on the river valley scenery.

In Painesville, the Gristmill and Millstone condominiums that were inundated by the July 2006 flood are scheduled for demolition. (They were finally torn down in 2013.) It has taken three years, but nine million dollars are committed by the state and federal governments to reimburse the people who lost their properties. Some of the money is to be used to turn the land into a passive park with trails through a grassy and forested area, but no amenities. Finally, people are catching on, although the same idea was proposed over one hundred years ago. There are still other homes, businesses, and apartments within the flood zone there, but this is a huge step in the right direction.

I have decided to stop studying the Grand River. I've accomplished my personal goal of paying more attention to the river although I have barely scratched the surface of available knowledge about it. And I didn't meet all my original goals. I didn't do an hour-long vigil in winter or at night. I still don't know the history of the bell tower in Walden II. I didn't canoe all the navigable sections of the river. I didn't watch a sunset or sunrise at the water's edge. And I regret that I forget to take photos at my usual sites on my 52nd visit and only got a few during the exciting 2006 flood.

I have witnessed an historical flood, a lesson to humanity in the larger scheme of things. All the people who lost homes in the flood know this planet will have its way with us. If this past season is the beginning of dramatic effects from globing warming that we, the population of the United States, are contributing to by our expanding and consuming ways, then there will be more storms and floods to come. New Orleans' devastation by Hurricane Katrina in 2005 will be predictive of similar events around the globe. Our friends out west will be migrating east for water. Our friends in Florida will be returning to the north for land. I'm going to stay right where I am and chronicle more about my property and local surroundings. I'm going to cut down on my consumerism (I could easily do with less), put my energies into electing responsible, forward-thinking leaders, and do more for the environment. Time is what I cherish along with my family and everything to do with nature. I love the Grand River more than ever; it is a piece of me after our year long affair. Long may its water flow.

July 27 – 28, 2006 flood

APPENDIX A

PROTECTED LANDS OF THE
GRAND RIVER WATERSHED

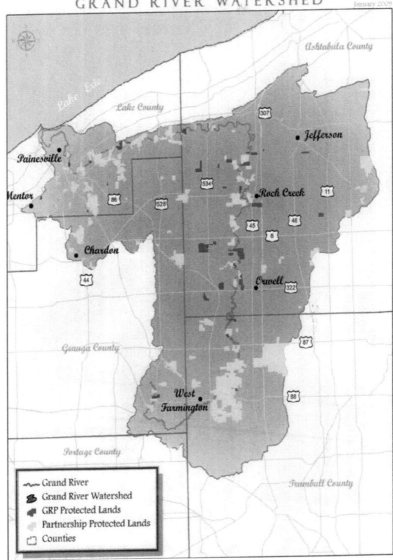

APPENDIX B

Major Tributaries of the Grand River
April 2009

Although I love my tattered 1985 Northeastern Ohio map for its road details, it does not display any of the Grand River's tributaries. There are 53 named streams (872 miles) that drain 712 square miles. I purchase a 2008 map; still the two tributaries that join to begin the river are not drawn, and many tributaries have their own tributaries, so I will limit my curiosity to only those that directly empty into the Grand River.

There are none in Geauga County. Trumbull County has Dead Branch, Mud Run, Center Creek, and Baughman Creek, all of which join the river inside the Grand River Wildlife Area near East Farmington. Farther north, Swine Creek (some of whose length was also named Plum Creek) merges with Anderson Creek. It is not clear which name goes with the merged water that ends at the river. Mill Creek is next, followed by Phelps Creek at Ashtabula County's border.

Moving north, the Hoskins and Indian creeks merge – not clear which name carries on – followed by Plumb Creek, Crooked Creek, Rock Creek, Three Brothers Creek (has to be a story there), Trumbull Creek, Branson Creek, and another Center Creek before the Grand River makes a ninety degree turn west. Coffee Creek flows into the river just after this bend, and then there are no tributaries shown on the map until Paine Creek enters just before the Vrooman Road crossing in Lake County. I know this is not accurate because Talcott Creek is in my township and before the Blair Road Bridge. My new Ohio map is useless and so is the 1997 Lake County map.

I go to the Geographic Information System (GIS) on Lake County's internet site. Even the hydrographic section does not name all the creeks. Does Talcott flow into another Mill Creek before the Grand River? After Mill Creek, is it Paine, Big, Kellogg and Red creeks before the Mentor Marsh drainage? I am off to see the large map on the wall outside the Grand River Partners' office. The streams drawn on it are also unnamed and the office is closed. I finally get help at the Lake County Soil and Water Conservation District office, where I copy pages from the Gazetteer of Lake County and get a 2007 county highway map.

Going back to the east end of Lake County, the first tributary is the second named Mill Creek. This one is only 3.03 miles long and enters through Hogback Ridge Lake Metropark. Next is Griswold Creek at the western edge of the Hidden Valley Metropark. Talcott Creek is next and the last one for many miles until the larger Paine Creek joins the river at Indian Point Metropark. However, the Gazetteer lists the Barber Ditch of 1.79 miles entering the river before the 7.48 mile Paine Creek. There is an unnamed blue line on the map too. Oh, my goodness, will I ever get this right?

Combining information from both the Gazetteer and the 2007 county map, I think the next tributaries are as follows: Tiber Creek, Big Creek, Hardy Creek, and Red Creek, as the river wends through Painesville and Fairport Harbor. Whew. Many sources state there are 53 named streams, but no one source lists them. I suspect I would have to look at each county's gazetteers to find all the names.

The Ohio Department of Natural Resources lists the principal streams as two in Ashtabula County (29.8 mile Mill Creek and 18.4 mile Rock Creek) and one in Lake County (15.8 mile Big Creek). Within these streams are 87 fish species and 26 mussel species. Lucky for you I cannot find a list of all of them, but I didn't try very hard.

It is only Lake County that has completed a Stream Sign Project. With private sponsors, a Cleveland Foundation grant, and signs and installation assistance by the Lake County Stormwater Management Department, 44 stream crossings have watershed signs. On green and white rectangles with some blue for water, the stream is named and its watershed district identified. The project was undertaken to "educate public about damaging non-point source pollution issues such as erosion and sedimentation", and to foster a "sense of ownership and protectiveness." These are excellent goals. Water health and riparian setbacks on the tributaries determine how pristine the Grand River will remain; they should be as revered as the river. Any water anywhere should concern us all.

APPENDIX C

Bridges over the Grand River

March 2009

It takes me 13 hours over two days and 121.9 miles to cross all 39 bridges over the 98.5 mile-long Grand River. The drive can be done in less time if you don't stop to take photos and record notes like I do. Some are only culverts, but *Webster's Dictionary* agrees with me – any structure built over a river, railroad, highway, etc. to provide a way across for vehicles or pedestrians is a bridge.

First though, I drive down Shedd Road (Parkman Township, Geauga County), hoping to view the river's southward beginnings, but all the small creeks here are flowing north through Amish farms. Although I assume the Amish's' land husbandry is gentler on the watershed – fewer fertilizers and pesticides – there are neither riparian setbacks nor fences around the creeks.

I consult my ragged 1985 Northeastern Ohio map for the route to the first river crossing – a map, as you will learn if you stick with reading this section – that is both a blessing and a curse. State roads will be designated by SR and national routes by U.S. All widths and heights are my approximations when source material is not found.

Bridge #1

On Nash Road, I am as close to the river's origin as I can get by car. The two unnamed creeks that merge to start the Grand River are on the Irwin farm somewhere north of this graveled road. Guard rails and yellow/black, diagonally-stripped highway signs mark the culvert's sides. There is no sign denoting the beginning of the mighty Grand River flowing under this road. The land around is gently rolling with the river in a slight dip between Amish farms and 'English' homes, as the Amish call everyone else.

Looking north, the four foot wide river snakes through shrubs and scattered deciduous trees. I see a small, private bridge and an outbuilding's roof – probably part of the residence on my right. Nearby, a singing red-winged blackbird helps mitigate the unwelcome sight of a white, plastic shopping bag caught in the downed brown grasses. Some new green grass blades reach for the clear skies. Looking south, I see a 500 foot-wide wetland bordered by wood with only some conifers' dark green needles relieving the overall brown. The river meanders through the middle of this wetland; its mud and gravel bottom visible, its babbling heard at surface stones.

I like calling this stream a river, because in my mind's eye I can visualize its track through five counties as it becomes a behemoth before draining into Lake Erie. Do the residents here know what this small waterway becomes? At the end of the wetland, about ¼ mile away, I see the next bridge. It's a good day to travel – warm enough to shed my fleece jacket – not bad for a March day in northeastern Ohio.

Bridge #2

SR 168 (Tavern Road or Warren-Burton Road) is also a large culvert signified by guardrails. The double-yellow center lines on the two lane paved road match the color of the warning rectangles attached to the rails' ends. The fifteen foot wide river flows ten feet below, burbling over medium-sized boulders in a small ravine. The view north into the wetland is partially obscured by eastern hemlocks among the bare deciduous trees along the river's east bank. There are farms here too, but far enough away that the river's habitat seems undisturbed. A sign for the Geauga Park District – access by permit only – helps explain that. On the southwest land, sap buckets hang on maple trees lining the river as it gently bends southeast.

Bridge #3

U.S. 422 (Main Market Road) is a four lane divided highway with a grass median strip on double bridges with low concrete side walls. I walk across the south bridge and stand with my knees against the cement barriers. Wind gusts from the heavy passing traffic push at my back. The ravine continues, but the surrounding land is hillier than at Tavern Road. The river, ten feet below, gently swishes between deciduous trees on both banks, sunlight sparkling on its ripples. Northeast, I see a house. Southwest, a large rectangular, flat-roofed industrial building jars the bucolic scene, but the river's passage here still feels separate and protected.

Bridge #4

I travel through the small town of Parkman and take SR 88 (Madison Road) to the bridge over one of the two remaining dams from the original four. This fifteen foot high concrete dam almost under the west edge of the steel and cement bridge has created a ½ mile long lake recently renamed Shrangri-La. Every time the clubhouse on the west shore is sold, the lake gets a new name – previously called Owen Pond, East Brook Dam, and Marsh Beach Club Lake. Today, an overturned canoe is the only hint of usage. Parkman's buildings are visible in the north. A pipe at the dam's north end spills water over tree limb debris into a narrow ravine with large boulders and wood. Birdsong abounds; a hawk circles above. Hidden among the trees on the southeast bank is the Stonewall Bed and Breakfast. The music of the rushing water through the boulder-strewn Grand River must sound lovely there.

Bridge #5

With the three previously described bridges circling Parkman, the Nelson Road Bridge is like the fourth spoke on a wheel. The 177.2 foot long concrete arch bridge was built around 1930 to span the end of the deep and narrow ravine that started at the dam upstream. Curving luxuriously south, high above the sparkling, rushing, thin water, it's a piece of art coming out of a dark forest to sunlight – totally unexpected next to a small town I know nothing about. I watch the river flow out of the ravine eastward onto flat land. Coltsfoots bloom along the road. Only a gravel lane angling east hints of human habitat although the town is just up the road.

Bridge #6

U.S. 422 (Main-Market Road again or Warren-Burton Road) has a brand new, four lane concrete bridge with a turn lane on its west edge for SR 282. A worker on a bulldozer molds the northwest embankment. Knee-high black plastic barriers are still in place along the river's banks. The busy traffic masks the river's gurgling water until I am standing directly over its flow on a wide berm mid-bridge. The bridge shadows the river coming from the southwest through a shallow valley. In the northeast, flatter land is flanked by campgrounds. A fifty foot barrier of vegetation and trees is on each bank. It's hard to enjoy the scene with constant traffic whizzing by.

Bridge #7

Hobart Road seems worlds away from busy U.S. 422. A two lane paved road crosses a culvert carrying the twenty-five foot wide river with its mild ripples and visible shale bottom approaching from the west. The surrounding land is treed and natural before farm fields begin. At the southeast end of the bridge, a gravel road heads east. I neither see nor hear any traffic. A roadside sign alerts drivers to watch for Amish buggies.

Bridge #8

At the Painesville-Warren or Old State Road crossing, farmland is all around, but rarely does any pasture extend to the three foot high muddy river banks. The two to three foot-deep river flows gently through a riparian setback of 100-150 feet. The nearest buildings are at least 500 feet away. The cement bottom bridge is railed by five rods on each side.

Bridge #9

The next bridge on Girdle Road has pastures to the river's banks on three sides. Cow paths are obvious on the sloping land; I hear mooing inside a large barn nearby. Although the pasture is fenced at the riverside and trees and some undergrowth cover about fifty percent of the banks, the river is vulnerable here. A horse and buggy pass by as I stand next to the guardrail. An Amish man in a motorized chair appears. "This is the Grand River, right?" I say. "I think so. Nice day again, huh?" he says. I am stunned. He must live nearby, and he is not sure of the river's name. He keeps moving. I am tempted to run after him and show him how on my map the Grand River squiggles past his road all the way north to Lake Erie, but I don't.

Bridge #10

At SR 534 the concrete bridge with its guardrails is just south of Farmington. I hear barking dogs and a crowing rooster. The town is primarily northwest, farmland southwest, but beginning eastward is the Grand River State Game Preserve. A sign in the dirt parking lot lists the preserve's hours. No vehicles are allowed, but hunting, fishing and trapping are permitted May 1 through August 31. On the sandbar along the northwest bank on the other side of the bridge it is very clear that ATVs have been driven to the river's edge. Otherwise the muddy waters are buffered by natural vegetation and trees. A covered bridge built here in 1867 was gone by 1925.

Bridge #11

Halfway between Farmington and East Farmington on SR 88, the next bridge lies inside the Grand River State Game Preserve. I walk past a dead skunk on my way to the middle of this culvert over gently flowing brown water with a hint of green. The flat land on all sides has wood and wetland, and in the north I see a thirty foot high bluff on the west side of the river as it bends out of sight. Previously at least four other roads (Norton, Hyde-Oakfield, Larson, and Peck) used to span the Grand River where the Preserve exists today. It's good vehicle access is limited, but this busy highway makes a lot of noise.

Bridge #12

It's ten miles north to SR 87 (the greatest distance between bridges so far) where I drive over many culverts before determining which one carries the Grand River. Trees and wetland exist on flat land as far as I can see. A roadside sign declares Wildlife Area. Is this still part of the game preserve or a separate site? I need a newer map. The fifty foot wide, quiet river approaches and departs in several channels. Tree debris piled against the southeast end of the bridge disturbs the water, creating the only sounds until I startle a pair of ducks into flight.

Bridge #13

To get to the next bridge, I take graveled Combs Road north through wetland pocked with trailers, small rundown homes and lots of trash.

When I reach the Road Closed sign, I decide to proceed assuming that the road doesn't end, but that travel is not advised in rainy springs. I am right. I maneuver my car around mud holes while enjoying the reappearance of the river on my right a sign reads Wildlife Area – 1 mile. The houses end. I see only a solitary silo and an abandoned gas/oil tank. The road ends next to the bridge on Donley Road surrounded by sycamore, beech and maple trees. Green grasses on the river's banks are all bent northward indicating higher water here recently. The water flows silently but birds and spring peepers sing. Flies, awakened by the day's warmth, buzz by. Although the concrete bridge is nondescript with its guardrail sides, this is a lovely secluded spot.

Bridge #14

At last, an older one lane bridge with crisscrossing three feet-high metal sides on a gravel road. This one on Old Plank Road (just over the county line in Ashtabula County) appears after driving past abandoned homes and trailers and a ½ mile stretch of harvested woods on the south side. The twenty feet wide Grand River is meandering through acres of branch and tree stump piles with mangled vegetation where logs were dragged to the road. One debris pile is being burnt, its smoke lazily curling upward. The river seems deep enough for boating. What would it be like to canoe out of the prior forest and enter this timbered area? At the bridge there is a small buffer of trees on both sides; however, a new home on the northeast bank has lawn to the river's edge. I like the rural seclusion and the weight limit sign for four different truck sizes before the fragile-looking bridge.

The original covered bridge at this site was destroyed by fire in the early 1970s. The county had no funds to replace the bridge so the road ended at the river. Because of the hardship this created for residents' travels and school bus schedules, a citizen's group formed and successfully got the National Guard to donate a used Bailey bridge – a welded pony, twin truss affair easily transported and assembled wherever a small bridge was needed. Installed over thirty years ago, it is no longer adequate for the traffic. But because of its background, the Bailey bridge has been deemed historical, and Ashtabula County has been requested to salvage the structure. It will be dissembled and moved to a county park for pedestrian use once federal funds become available to build a new metal truss bridge. I'm glad I got to drive across the old Bailey bridge.

Bridge # 15

Next is the busy U.S. 322 Bridge. This concrete one with only guardrail sides is about one hundred feet long. The thirty foot-wide muddy river flows silently between flat wetland and farmland, some of it fallow. This bridge has a sign that reads Grand State Scenic River. Wow, is that confusing – how could you ever figure out that it was the Grand River from that sequence of words? There was another sign with the same verbiage in my county. Someone must have complained because now the sign reads Grand River on the top line, Wild and Scenic River on the second line. Now that makes sense.

Bridge #16

Driving slowly downhill on the straight, paved New Hudson Road, I find a 170 foot-long, large, galvanized steel truss bridge with spanning girders overhead. Built in 1925, the arch bridge is beautiful and perfect for this setting with the tree-buffered Grand River flowing past in its thirty foot wide channel. Beyond are scattered farms. There are no signs for bridge height or weight limits, just the bare metal fanned struts in groups of three rising to the height of the top curving arches. Long may this bridge reign.

Bridge #17

The next bridge on Montgomery Road is similar to the last one. A seventy-five foot-long, galvanized steel, arching structure, its three grouped trusses on its side fanning downward instead of up. It is one-half the height of the previous bridge. It seems only wide enough for one vehicle, but a two lane paved road leads to and from it. The thirty foot wide, twisting, muddy Grand River flows gently and quietly in a slight valley with natural vegetation on both banks. Farms can be seen east and west. Coltsfoots bloom along the road. After taking my photos, I hurry to move my car closer to the bridge so two men in a truck can back out of a lane on the southwest leading to an oil/gas tank. They say hello as the truck lumbers to and over the bridge. I like how this road curves to enter or exit the bridge which was aligned with the river. Anyone coming this way has to slow down and maybe see the river.

Bridge #18

Oh, wow, another spectacular bridge awaits me on Johnson Road. This 128 foot- long Pratt through-truss bridge is made of green metal and everything about it is squared or rectangular. Two foot high girders with fretwork span the top like widely spaced strips of lace above the thirteen and a half foot clearance. Built in 1905 by the King Bridge Company, it frames a two lane paved road as it crosses the twenty-five foot wide Grand River flowing in a recently flooded dip in the land. The soiled grasses and muddied tree trunks indicate the water rose about ten feet. I watch the passage of a short stick on the water and estimate its speed at two feet per second. Farms can be seen on the flat lands east and west. The bridge squeaks and snaps as I drive over it. At the first house beyond the tall pines on the southeast, a woman, intent on pulling weeds from among her crocuses, doesn't look up as I pass by. The pavement soon stops, and I travel on a sometimes spongy gravel road between wet woods and past a High Water Area sign.

Bridge #19

U.S. 6 is another busy road with one of those weirdly-labeled river name signs before the low-sided concrete bridge with metal guardrails. The fifty foot-wide river flows between 400 feet of natural vegetation. Surrounding the small valley are scattered homes and farms on slightly rolling hills. The big news here is the Grand River Jersey Farm Canoe Access Site on the southeast. An open patch of land with a gravel turnabout has a steep, brief path to the bridge's edge for river access. A big sign lists the participating sponsors: Grand River Jersey Farms, Ohio Department of Natural Resources, Ohio Department of Health, and Grand River Partners. Folks around here sure can't miss that this is an important river.

Bridge # 20

First I try to reach the river on Laskey Road, but there is no east egress off Mechanicsville Road. I stop to ask a man rototilling his garden soil what happened to the rest of Laskey Road. "How old is that map? That end of Laskey has been gone for years," he says. On I motor to Callender Road and find a 253 foot-long, green metal bridge built in 1913 – a Pratt through-truss bridge with plate girder spans. V-lacing fretwork adorns the top girders and end posts. Additional low, green metal barriers on both sides lead to the 15.1 foot wide bridge. A height limit sign (7 feet 0 inches) is suspended on cables overhead. What is unusual about this bridge is its skewed portal view. Under the bridge, the full and muddy river is even wider, its flow almost imperceptible. All is quiet on the surrounding lands with its trees and scattered homes. Some lawn comes to the river on the southeast. The sporadic rat-a-tat-tats of woodpeckers interrupt the stillness. A gravel road leads northwest along the river with a sign for the Grand Valley Christian Center. It's nice to be back on a quiet road with an old large metal bridge.

Bridge # 21

The next bridge on Shaffer Road is even better. It's a one lane gravel road through another green metal bridge with overhead girders also built in 1913 after that year's March flood destroyed a covered bridge – probably the longest single span one in Ashtabula County at that time. The current 168 foot-long bridge is only marred by those black and yellow diagonally striped highway barrier signs, as if you couldn't see this big bridge and its guardrail entrances, even at night. Described as an eight panel Pratt through-truss, this bridge was restored and new modern railings added in 2001. In the south the river has expanded to 120 feet as it flows in two channels around a small, treed island. Branches, hanging in the muddy water, explain the bubbling. The recent high water stayed within the small valley created by the river, not reaching the old farmhouses on three sides. In the north the river narrows to seventy-five feet, flowing through a wooded area with hemlocks on a fifty foot high bluff. Once again quiet reigns, except for birdsong in sunlight under blue skies. This is the sixth 'erector set' type bridge and the fifth taller than me.

Bridge #22

On Richmond Road, the 150 foot-long bridge is a modern one with one metal railing on its low, concrete sides. The two lane paved road is flat, hiding the fact that the land dips to accommodate the seventy-five foot wide Grand River whose brown water flows quietly north with some eddies around some submerged trees. Farmland starts after the fifty feet riparian setback. Wider flood zones and more trees are seen in the north before the river sharply bends out of sight.

Bridge # 23

It's a covered bridge I see as I come down a curvy hill from the east into a small, wooded valley on Riverdale Road. Dark brown, creosote-soaked vertical wood boards are topped by a just-barely-red roof. The 113.9 foot-long and twelve and a half foot-wide, one lane, town lattice bridge with wooden floors and ceiling was built in 1900 and has a 9 foot, 6 inch clearance. I walk inside the bridge to touch the large trusses that are over one hundred years old. Some structural gaps on both sides admit light and river views. Through five human generations, this bridge has spanned this river, which today is huge and muddy with sonorous sloshing around the submerged tree trunks. What a treasure.

Bridge #24

My old map shows a crossing on Fobes Road. A No Outlet sign at the road's west entrance predicts the bridge is gone, but I can't resist going to see where it used to be. I pass one residence about ¼ mile in before the road ends at a stop sign perched on large rectangular stones. I walk 150 feet down a sloping old roadbed to the river's edge. The valley is wide here and completely wooded as far as I can see. The broad river is full and lapping only as it goes around two rusting metal foundation trusses in its middle. What a great place to river watch or start a boat trip. I leave reluctantly for the next bridge on Sweitzer Road (as the map spells it) or Schweitzer Road (as its sign reads). Hurrah, it's another metal bridge, this time gray and not-so-high but about 150 feet long in a small, wooded valley with no visible houses. This Warren truss low-pony configuration (meaning it has no overhead cross beams) was constructed of galvanized steel in 1966. I hear river sounds in the north, but under the two lane paved road, the deep and wide water runs soundlessly. Coltsfoots bloom along the road, birds sing, and two vultures circle in the blue sky with its few wispy clouds. Although I would have liked to have seen the destroyed Fobes Road covered bridge and don't regret that its access is gone, this bridge is just as great. Just east on both sides of the road is a 695 acre preserve called Grand River Terraces. The surrounding wetland with flood plain meadows, ponds, and swamp forests depends on the rising and falling water of the Grand River to maintain its diversity of plants, many of which are threatened and endangered species, such as dewdrops. Because the river used to run much higher than it does today, the terraces inhibited grazing animals. It is a pleasure to travel slowly through this area and hear birdsong – nearly one hundred bird species have been sighted here.

Bridge #25

Cold Springs Road (I wonder where the springs are) crosses the Grand River on a modern, low concrete-sided bridge with very white sides. Wood and wetland surround two home sites tucked back on the southeast; I hear talking. Northeast and northwest around the one hundred foot wide, silently flowing muddy river, all is nature. On the southwest is a tidy farm with many white buildings. I suspect the mowed lawn to the river's edge used to be pasture. Only scattered, mature trees anchor the muddy bank there. The river flows by thirty feet below the bridge's bottom.

Bridge #26

Before I drive to the next bridge on Mechanicsville Road, I stop at the sites of two former river crossings. Tote Road is now an Austinburg Township park to the river's edge. Pelton Road is a cul-du-sac with houses nestled in trees about 200 feet back from the water. No remnant of either bridge remains.

The next bridge is a 160.1-foot long covered span built in 1867. 1867! This Burr Arch truss bridge has been here 142 years. A refurbishment in 2003 assured many more years of service. The longest, single span covered bridge in Ohio, the all-wood bridge with a red roof is painted beige. A long line of unplanked trusses on both sides allow river views from inside. Strings of small lights outline open-air windows, and a star-shaped frame with lights hangs over the one window under the roof at the western entrance. A sign prohibits trucks and buses from crossing the bridge, but right next to it on the northern arm of a Y-shaped road is a newer, two lane concrete bridge with low guardrail sides. So every car approaching this small valley must choose which bridge to cross. I suspect it depends on which way one plans to turn at Lampson Road once over the river. I would choose to cross the covered bridge every time just to hear my tires rumble on the wood floor and see the one hundred foot wide rustling waterway below, as full as its banks will allow. Two cars pass me in the bridge while I am taking photos. We wave and smile.

Northwest across the road is the Grand River Manor established 1847 – twenty years before the covered bridge was built. Was it a ferry site? A screened-in eating porch and picnic tables scattered on its lawn face the river. This looks like a great place to eat - I will come back. I notice on the map that the Grand River is now flowing west after a sharp bend before the Tote Road Township Park.

Bridge #27

I am now near the beginnings of what is known as the gorge area of the Grand River. At SR 534, a wide, two lane, 200 foot-long concrete bridge crosses a deep valley. The signage again reads Grand State Scenic River. Oh, dear. From the east comes the 200 foot-wide, slowly moving, silent, brown river from around a gentle bend. North is a treed bluff with one home perched at its edge. In the west the river broadens even more behind a dam just before the next covered bridge.

Bridge #28

I am at the Harpersfield Covered Bridge, an Ashtabula County MetroPark and National Register of Historic Places' site. Two joined bridges span 368 feet just east of the fifteen foot-high dam on State Road. The 140 foot-long, green metal truss bridge on the north side has a height limit of 12 feet, 9 inches. It is connected to a 228 foot-long, weathered wood, covered bridge, whose height limit sign reads 10 feet, 9 inches. Truckers need to be looking ahead when approaching this crossing. Originally the whole span was a covered bridge built in 1868 to replace another bridge that was washed away. This covered bridge is described as a two span, wooden Howe truss bridge with center pier and was the longest covered bridge in the state until a 613 foot-long one was built in 2008 farther north over the Ashtabula River. In the 1913 flood, the northern half of the covered bridge here was washed away and replaced with the metal one existing today. In 1992, a walkway was added on the west side of the covered bridge during its rehabilitation.

I walk the walkway, feel the bridge shake as vehicles pass behind me, and hear the roaring water from the dam in the east and the swooshing of the mild rapids in the west. Froth and foam covers fifty percent of the water's surface. Other tourists pass me on the walkway.

Two men are fishing from crooked foundation stones on the southeast corner. One canoeist and one kayaker enter the river near the gentle westward bend. I could stand here for a long time, but other bridges beckon.

Bridge #29

After traveling seven miles parallel to the river past vineyards on South River Road, I approach the next crossing at County Line Road, the border between Ashtabula and Lake counties. Just before the river valley at the end of flat land on the narrow gravel road is a sign on the east side for the Cash/Hetrick Preserve. The Cleveland Museum of Natural History owns this property in memory of Jerry Case and John Hetrick "who championed the preservation of natural lands."

Driving down the curvy and steep gravel road between water-eroded sides, I come to the Clyde Hill Road Bridge – the old and more poetic name for this road. Two joined bridges, one historic and one modern, span 259.9 feet across the river. The north half was built in 1889 – a large, green metal rectangular-shaped structure with fretwork on its ceiling girders that allow a fifteen foot clearance. Erected in 2002 by Ashtabula County, the south metal bridge with its arching sides and no overhead girders (modern pony truss) is half the height of the Pratt one and replaced a prior wooden pony truss bridge that was washed away. I remember this road being closed and only the 1889 bridge standing when I first canoed the river years ago.

Except for two houses on the north side (one on flood-prone land next to the water's edge and one halfway up the northeast hill), the area is heavily wooded with bluffs on both sides. Standing on the first bridge I see the canoeist and kayaker who entered the river at Harpersfield. We call greetings to each other and remark on the lovely day. They tell me about a Canada goose nest on the small island behind them. I watch as they rarely drop a paddle into the fast-flowing, faintly-rippled brown water before going out of sight on a gentle westward bend.

Bridge #30

I am now in Lake County, my county, and I know the bridges will be farther apart. The next one at SR 528 has the aforementioned corrected signage. I am not walking out on this bridge; the two lane paved road is a busy one, and there is less than three feet between the traffic's lanes and the low concrete walls topped by mesh fencing. This is a valley jumper bridge built in 1962 from the top I drive below the bridge to the Hidden Valley Metropark.

In 1893 two iron bridges were built by the King Bridge Company of Cleveland to span the broad river here. All that remains now of the

Bailey Road Bridge are two twelve foot high stacked stone pilings east in the middle of the river. On the first concrete piling in the river for the existing high level bridge are black etched lines and numbers for measuring the water's depth in feet. Today the river's flow reaches the four foot line, but the numbers go up to twelve. To the right on the same piling, someone has drawn in chalk a crude tower with an up arrow at its top. I wonder what that is all about. This is a canoe takeout point for the liveries that ply their trade on this section of the Grand River. Although the river murmurs, it has to compete with traffic overhead on the blue bottomed bridge. Clunking sounds fill the valley as each vehicle passes over the bridge's metal seams of the south bluff to the north bluff about 200 feet above the river.

Bridge #31

To get to the next crossing, I drive north and then west on Interstate 90. I doubt I will be able to get photos but I am in luck. These side-by-side 400 foot-long bridges, built ninety-five feet above the river in 1959, are being replaced because their construction is similar to the bridge that collapsed in Minneapolis recently. Traffic continues on reinforced trusses as new bridges are being built right next to the old ones.

It is Sunday so I drive off the road onto a gravel path lined with parked construction equipment. I stop my car at the top of a steep descent and walk down to the pilings at the river's edge. Here the water heads north between valley walls and temporary wood/plastic barriers. The green metal trusses on lower concrete pilings will be gone, and new all-concrete pilings will stretch up a hundred feet to the new roadbeds. It's hard to imagine that the scars caused by this work will be eradicated, but eventually the valley will be allowed to proceed below the bridge as nature intended. Meanwhile the brown waters of the Grand River whisper pass the mess; dark green hemlock needles the only color in the surrounding woods.

Bridge # 32

The Blair Road Bridge is next, and I don't drive there today since it's the site I visited weekly. I have miles to go still and I want to reach the last bridge before the sun sets. However, I will relate what I learned about the $95,000 repair completed October 2008. The water erodes the loose mortar joints between the stones that have been there for over 140 years, and the 40 foot-long northeast wing wall starts leaning toward the river. This is the second such repair since I started this book in 2004. The Grand River can be a challenge for engineers.

Bridge #33

One of the two remaining metal truss bridges in Lake County is next at Vrooman Road. The valley is wide here with the river flowing closer to the north wall. Two identical, pale green, arching metal bridges join to span the 200 foot-wide river, accepting traffic from SR 84 up on the north ridge and funneling it toward Interstate 90. Mason's Landing Metropark comes to the river's edge on the northwest corner. A canoe launching ramp, picnic tables, and ½ mile hiking trail attract people here. Fishermen tend to park on the gravel berm southeast of the bridge just before the entrance to Indian Point Metropark. Because of predictable flooding here with any heavy rainstorm, which reroutes a lot of vehicles trying to get to Interstate 90, money has been designated to replace this bridge. The final plans have not been announced, but the proposed options of either a high level valley jumper bridge like the one at SR 528 or a lower one (but obviously higher than the existing one) are both meeting with opposition. There are Indian burials in the area; Lake Metroparks doesn't want its land overrun; the electric company has high wire towers spanning the valley; and residents don't want their curvy, narrow, two lane road turned into a wider, straighter, faster path to the freeway. I would prefer (as do the Grand River Partners) the lower level bridge so that travelers at least can see the river in all its phases. Already, a flood stage marker on the northeast edge of the bridge is gone. I miss seeing its reminder of the heights that flood waters can reach here.

Bridge #34

The next bridge on East Walnut Street (SR 84) in Painesville is a new bridge (2005) that the powers-that-be almost got right. It's long, gently bent on seven concrete pilings, and wide with pedestrian walks, but the river cannot be seen from a car – the view is blocked by concrete sides and guardrails. Because the east and west roads both go downhill, the whole valley with its bridge is plainly visible then, but for full views at the river, one has to park on a paved pullout on the southwest edge. I hear the river splashing over boulders and tree debris. For an urban setting, this still feels wild, open and natural.

After curving west to north, the river twists and turns, one wide channel against the west bluff with its line of houses, another one angling farther east under the Norfolk and Southern Railroad trestle also spanning this valley. The house on the northwest side is up an embankment but its lawn extends to the riverbed. Ten Canada geese are plucking at the first grass shoots there. Beyond the house, the land rises rapidly. Lake County's newest Metropark, Beaty Landing, has an entrance halfway up the west hill.

The next bridge in Painesville crosses the Grand River at Main Street. Here the southwest bluff is higher, abruptly ending at the road. The other three sides are lowlands and flood plains which have been covered in all major floods. The low-sided concrete and guardrail bridge takes off from the west hill and curves slightly south. The river can be seen as one drives across this bridge and it is impressive, all its force compressed against the western bluff as water turns to run across the valley floor. It rumbles and thunders in and around pilings holding caught flotsam. This section of the river is not runable by canoe or kayak – portage is recommended.

Painesville Kiwanis Recreation Park's picnic areas and ball fields occupy most of the northwest bank. I find a worn path just off the park's driveway going through grasses, shrubs and trees to under the bridge where a fifty foot wide, well-trod earth berm exists. Huge concrete chunks and old foundation stones along with a log jam explain the accumulated soil. Colorful graffiti everywhere suggests this secluded spot is used. It certainly could shelter homeless people from rain and snow.

The prior metal truss bridge here (350 feet long and fifty-five feet high) was significant because of the size of the Pennsylvania style pin connected-through-truss. Right! And it replaced a covered bridge that existed from 1866 until 1896. The first bridge ever over the Grand River was built by Joel Scott in 1806 at New Market, which was somewhere around here, but I have been unable to pinpoint the exact location. This town, Painesville, now has a mall named New Market. I wonder what future bridges will look like. No matter; somebody needs to pick up the trash here and remove or paint over the graffiti. I don't have a garbage bag with me, and it's getting late.

Bridge #36

The river is meandering north through Painesville on its eastern edge. The next bridge on Erie Street (U.S. 20) has the city all around but little in evidence. This modern concrete bridge opened for traffic on October 6, 1988. The river's east bluff shows scars from earth slides. A factory, Eckart Effect Pigments, fills the flatland on the southwest edge. Its buildings are tidy-whitey, and the grounds neatly manicured down to the river. On the northern sides, east and west, all is woods up to and under the old arched-concrete 350 foot long railroad viaduct (built one hundred feet above the river in 1908). Beyond this CSX railroad bridge, I can see the double low-level, concrete SR 2 bridges about ½ mile away.

As I return to my car parked northeast of the bridge, I watch a van pull in and park on a short abandoned roadway just beyond. A man and woman carrying paper bags exit the van, cross U.S. 20, and run along the railroad bridge embankment. They are quickly out of sight among the shrubs. Rumor has it that the homeless live in the sheltered tunnels formed by the bridges' arches.

Bridge #37

The only photo I get from the side of the road on very busy SR 2 is of the two low, concrete-sided spans carrying four lanes of traffic across the Grand River. There is no room for anyone to walk on the bridges, nor would I want to. The river flows north in a small valley with natural vegetation. I am glad to get back in the car and safely merge with the fast and thick traffic.

Bridge #38

The next bridge on North St. Clair Street is a totally different experience. I drive from the bluff at the end of Painesville over a straight, modern, low-level concrete bridge into Fairport Harbor on the flatland beyond. The river is broader, full, and silently but rapidly flowing westward after a bend upstream just beyond the water treatment plant. Houses perch along the south bluff downstream, but across the river on the northwest bank is another Lake County Metropark called Grand River Landing A small boat ramp is available for only canoes or kayaks because the low bridge downstream precludes taller watercraft. Picnic tables dot the eighteen grassy acres next to a small parking lot. This would be a great place to watch the river or fish or dream or blanket-nap.

Bridge #39

I arrive at the last vehicle bridge over the Grand River on Richmond Street, again a boundary between Painesville and Fairport Harbor. The one hundred foot wide watercourse still flows west, but a bend downstream beyond the black girder railroad bridge just on the other side of this low-level, concrete, two lane one directs the river north to Lake Erie. Here is where all the boat docks start. The traffic is heavy, and the bridge has no room for pedestrians, so I drive up the southeast hill to a new housing development to get a photo. While homes do exist here, they perch above the flood zones and wetland. Not so for the buildings on the northeast and northwest. They are on the flatlands which floods when this river cannot contain all the water it receives along its 98.5-mile, snakelike journey through five counties. However, Lake Erie can and does accept all water coming its way. It's 4:30 p.m. – cold and windy just two miles from the lake. I'm going home for some hot chocolate and dinner.

Of the thirty-nine bridges I crossed, seven are in rural Geauga County, six in rural northern Trumbull County, sixteen on the back roads of Ashtabula County, and ten in Lake County's rural bluff/valley settings to finally urban areas. Only fifteen percent (six) of the bridges have signs naming the Grand River. I counted eight locations that no longer have bridges. There were probably even more at one time, maybe ones never printed on any map. If one includes the four railroad bridges, all of which are in Painesville or Fairport Harbor, the river crossings total forty-two now. Hopefully, the future holds even fewer bridges, or at least ones that do no harm and let you see the river.

SELECTED RESOURCES

Books and Periodicals

- Albrecht, Brian. "Bear encounters in Ohio becoming more common," *The Plain Dealer,* May 4, 2006.
- Atassi, Leila; Dissell, Rachel; Martin, Maggie; Scott, Michael; Farkas, Karen. "Rain and fury," *The Plain Dealer*, July 29, 2006.
- *Birds of North America*, Fred J. Alsop III in association with the Smithsonian Institution 2002, DK Publishing, Inc., NY, NY.
- Crow, Kim. "After the STORM," *The Plain Dealer*, November 1, 2006.
- Feather, Carl E. "Forgotten Crossings of the Grand," *Star Beacon*, March 28, 2009.
- "Fit for a queen: Unwanted, invasive sea lampreys from Great lakes shipped to England for pie," *Detroit Free Press*, April 27, 2012.
- *Flood of 1913*, Ohio Historical Society, 1982 Velma Ave., Columbus, OH 43211.
- Forsyth, Jane L. "The Beach Ridges of Northern Ohio," Information Circular No. 25, State of Ohio, Division of Geological Survey, Columbus, 1959.
- Galbincea, Pat. "Blue skies will come again,...," *The Plain Dealer*, February 18, 2010.
- *Geauga, A Magazine for the County*, Spring 2008, pg. 33.
- Horton, John. "Ashtabula County covered bridge will be nation's longest," *The Plain Dealer,* August 22, 2008.
- Keany, Luaundra. "20 Things You Didn't Know About Light," *Discover*, 31(2), 2010, P.80.
- Kuehner, John C. "River poisoning intentional, meant to kill lamprey," *The Plain Dealer*, April 7, 2006.
- Litt, Steven. "House of Their Dreams is a Frank Lloyd Wright," *The Plain Dealer*, May 6, 2007.
- Marmolya, Gary Allen. <u>Gems of the Necklace</u>, Images of the Cleveland Metropolitan Parks, Photographs Elite, Cleveland, Ohio, 1993.
- Martin, Maggie. "Lake County flood haunts its victims," *The Plain Dealer*, July 28, 2007.
- Obmascik, Mark. <u>The Big Year, A Tale of Man, Nature, and Fowl Obsession</u>. Free Press, New York, NY, 2004.

- Ostrander, Stephen, Ed. *The Ohio Nature Almanac, An Encyclopedia of Indispensable Information About the Natural Buckeye Universe*, Orange Frazer Press, Wilmington, Ohio, 2001.
- Sangiacomo, Michael. "Painesville to buy, raze Gristmill condos," T*he Plain Dealer*, November 5, 2007.
- Schmidlin, Thomas W., "Climatic Summary of Snowfall and Snow Depth in the Ohio Snowbelt at Chardon," *Ohio Journal of Science*, 89(4):101-108, 1989.
- "Shakes, rattles, & quakes in NE Ohio," *The Plain Dealer*, January 31, 2006.
- Scott, Michael, "From condos to parkland: $9 million," *The Plain Dealer*, March 12, 2009.
- Scott, Michael. "Once nearly extinct, Ohio bald eagles thrive," *The Plain Dealer*, January 25, 2008.
- Snook, Debbi. "Peaceful passages, Ashtabula County covers more bridges," *The Plain Dealer*, October 11, 1998.
- "The Flood of July 2006," *LeRoy Dispatch*, Issue 3 of 2006.
- The Lake County Historical Society, <u>Here Is Lake County, Ohio</u>. Howard Allen, Inc., Publishers, Cleveland, Ohio, 1964.
- *The Painesville Telegraph*, September 8, 1974.
- *The Telegraph = Republican*, March 22-March 26, 1913, May 15, 17, and 24, 1893.
- *Volunteer Update*, The Volunteer Newsletter of the Ohio Chapter of the Nature Conservancy, Autumn 2003.
- Warsinskey, Tim. "The Grand River from Beginning to End." *The Plain Dealer SUNDAY MAGAZINE*, September 6, 1998, The Plain Dealer Publishing Co., Cleveland, OH 44114, 1998.
- White, Mel. *National Geographic Guide to Birdwatching Sites Eastern U.S.* 1999, p. 290-291.
- 1996 Appointment Calendar, Lake County—Then and Now. Lake County Historical Society, Printed in U.S.A.

Agencies

- Lake County Engineer, <u>www.lakecountyohio.org</u>
- Lake County Metroparks, <u>www.lakemetroparks.com</u>
- Lake County Soil and Water Conservation District, Painesville, OH. <u>www.lakecountyohio.org</u>
- National Geographic Society, Washington, D.C., <u>www.nationalgeographic.ocm</u>

- Ohio Department of Natural Resources, Division of Natural Areas and Preserves, www.dnr.state.oh.us
- Ohio Nature Conservancy, www.nature.org/ohio
- Western Reserve Land Conservancy, www.wrlandconservancy.org
- U.S. Department of Interior, www.doi.gov
- U.S. Environmental Protection Agency (EPA), www.epa.gov

Internet Sites

- Animal Life Spans, A Chart for Quick Reference, www.suite101*.com
- Ashtabula County, Ohio Convention and Visitors Bureau, www.visitashtabulacounty.com
- Audubon Society of Ohio, www.audubon.org/chapter/oh
- Birdwatcher's Digest, www.birdwatchersdigest.com
- Buckeye Trail Association, P.O. Box 254, Worthington, Ohio 43085, info@buckeyetrail.org
- Charles Whittlesey. Ohio History Central, A product of the Ohio Historical Society, 2009. www.ohiohistorycentral.org
- Cleveland Museum of Natural History, www.cmnh.org
- First American Flood Data Services, www.floodinsights.com
- Grand River Bridges in Northeastern Ohio, www.venangoil.com/bridgesohiogran.html
- Grand River Canoe Livery, www.grandrivercanoelivery.com
- Grand River – Wikipedia, http://en.wikipedia.org/wiki/Grand River
- Historic Bridges of the U.S., www.bridgehunter.com
- Ice – Wikipedia, http://en.wikipedia.org/wiki/Ice
- Memory Project, www.clevelandmemory.org
- Mountain Zone, www.mountainzone.com
- *Platanus occidentalis* – Wikipedia, http://en.wikipedia.org/wiki/Plantanus_occidentalis
- Pre-Recorded History of the Watershed", Northeast Ohio Areawide Coordinating Agency, www.noaca.org.
- Raccoon Run Canoe Rental, www.raccoonruncanoerental.com
- Rich Exner, Plain Dealer Computer Assisted Reporting Editor, "Sunny and Cloudy U.S. Places," August 12, 2008: "Cleveland snowfall totals year by year," May 27, 2009, www.cleveland.com/datacentral

- Saint Joseph Vineyard, www.saintjosephvineyard.com
- "The Beaver (Castor Canadensis)," *All about Beavers*, www.beaversww.org
- The Cleveland Mountain Zone, www.mountainzone.com
- The Winegrowers of the Grand River Valley, www.winegrowersofgrv.com

Miscellaneous

- Alex Bevan/Fiddler's Wynde Music BMI, www.ncweb.com/ent/alex
- GIS (Geographical Information System), Lake County, OH.
- Rose Moore, Reporter, Gazette publishers.
- "Great Floods: The Entire Nation, March 1913, Grand River, July, 2006," Speech by Librarians of Morley Library, Painesville, Ohio, 2006.
- *Watersongs*, Alex Bevan/ Fiddler's Wynde Music BMI, 1990, www.AlexBevan.com
- U.S. Geological Survey, In cooperation with the Federal Emergency Management Agency, "Flood of July 27-31, 2006 on the Grand River near Painesville, Ohio," by Andrew D. Edner, James M. Sherwood, Brian Astifan, and Kirk Lombardy, Open-File Report 2007-1164.

ACKNOWLEDGEMENTS

I was surprised by and grateful for the generous people who consented to be interviewed or freely answered my telephone and email queries for this book. Not only did they willingly share their experiences and knowledge, but they want to buy a copy of the completed book. It seems lots of people in northeast Ohio are excited by the Grand River and love talking about it. Any mistakes are my own, but feel free to point them out.

Not enough can be said for my readers, starting with Jackie Evangelista, who read my pages twice. Her comments on overall structure were immensely helpful. Gretchen Reed got out a red pen leftover from her English-teaching career and whipped my word use and grammar into place. Colby Dyer, the engineer, found any questionable facts and figures, while lauding my accomplishment. What more could one ask of a husband. George Warnock, from the Western Reserve Land Conservancy where Grand River Partners ended up, shared his expertise where I missed or muddled details. I'm especially grateful because he is so busy; you should check out what all the Conservancy is doing for this part of the world. And finally, my close friend, Dona Riczinger, moved back to Ohio just when I needed a push to revise my pages one more time. Her prior experience as an editor brought everything together.

I owe a debt to any and all acquaintances who upon learning of my project could not keep a look of skepticism off their faces. It kept me going because I wanted to show them I could write a book. They still may not love the book, but at least there may be a different expression upon their faces when I sell them a copy. And if after reading it, my friends decide to write their own books – because if she did it, I can too – then hurray for us all.

ABOUT THE AUTHOR

Margie DeLong is a retired nurse practitioner who always wrote on the side. Although she has had a few poems and essays published, this is her first book. A grandmother of five children, she resides in LeRoy Township with her husband.